THE ROMAN RITUAL

RENEWED BY DECREE OF
THE MOST HOLY SECOND ECUMENICAL COUNCIL OF THE VATICAN
AND PROMULGATED BY AUTHORITY OF POPE PAUL VI

THE ORDER OF
BAPTISM OF CHILDREN

ENGLISH TRANSLATION ACCORDING
TO THE SECOND TYPICAL EDITION

For Use in the Dioceses of the United States of America

Approved by the
United States Conference of Catholic Bishops
and Confirmed by the Apostolic See

2020

Concordat cum originali:
✝ Wilton D. Gregory
Chairman, USCCB Committee on Divine Worship
after review by Rev. Andrew Menke
Executive Director, USCCB Secretariat of Divine Worship

Published by authority of the Committee on Divine Worship,
United States Conference of Catholic Bishops

This book was edited by Danielle A. Noe. Christian Rocha was the production editor, Anna Manhart was the cover designer, and Mark Hollopeter adapted the interior design and was the production artist.

THE ORDER OF BAPTISM OF CHILDREN © 2020 Archdiocese of Chicago: Liturgy Training Publications, 3949 South Racine Avenue, Chicago, IL 60609; 800-933-1800; fax: 800-933-7094; email: orders@ltp.org; website: www.LTP.org. All rights reserved.

24 23 22 21 20   1 2 3 4 5

Printed and bound in the United States of America

ISBN 978-1-61671-418-5
OBCRE

LITURGY
TRAINING
PUBLICATIONS

CONTENTS

SACRED CONGREGATION FOR DIVINE WORSHIP

Prot. n. 50/69

DECREE

The Second Vatican Council decreed that the current *Ordo Baptismi parvulorum* in the Roman Ritual should be revised, in order that the rite might be adapted to the actual condition of children; the role and responsibilities of parents and godparents might be more clearly expressed; suitable adaptations might be made for the Baptism of a large number, or for Baptism to be celebrated by catechists, in missionary areas, or by others, in the absence of the ordinary minister; and that an *Ordo* might be provided to show that an infant, baptized according to the shorter rite, has already been received into the Church (Constitution on the Sacred Liturgy, nos. 67–69).

This revision has been carried out by the Consilium for the Implementation of the Constitution on the Sacred Liturgy. By his apostolic authority the Supreme Pontiff PAUL VI has approved the new *Ordo Baptismi parvulorum* to be used in the future in place of the existing *Ordo* in the Roman Ritual and has ordered its publication.

Therefore this Sacred Congregation, by special mandate of the same Supreme Pontiff, promulgates it, directing that it be used from September 8, 1969.

All things to the contrary notwithstanding.

From the offices of the Sacred Congregation for Divine Worship, May 15, 1969, Solemnity of the Ascension of the Lord.

BENNO Cardinal GUT
Prefect

A. BUGNINI
Secretary

SACRED CONGREGATION FOR DIVINE WORSHIP

Prot. n. 516/73

PREFACE TO THE SECOND EDITION

Since it was necessary that the *Ordo Baptismi parvulorum*, published in 1969, should be reprinted, it seemed opportune to produce a second edition of the *Ordo*, with certain variants and additions. The more important are as follows:

1. page 7, no. 2 [page 1 in this edition]:
   in place of "a nativa hominum condicione" ("from their natural human condition") is said: "de potestate tenebrarum erepti" ("rescued from the power of darkness");

2. page 8, no. 5: [page 2 in this edition]:
   after the word "homines" ("human beings") is added: "ab omni culpæ labe, tum originali tum personali, abluit eosque . . . " ("of every stain of sin, both original and personal");

3. page 15, no. 1 [page 9 in this edition]:
   the words "habere et" ("have or") are deleted;

4. page 85, no. 221 [page 124 in this edition]:
   in place of "a potestate tenebrarum," ("out of the power of darkness") is said: "ab originalis culpæ labe nunc" ("now from the stain of Original Sin").

Certain other variants of lesser importance have been introduced into the headings and rubrics, so that they may correspond better with the words and phrases that occur in liturgical books published since 1969.

The Sacred Congregation for Divine Worship now issues this second edition of the *Ordo Baptismi parvulorum*, which by his authority the Supreme Pontiff PAUL VI has approved, and declares it to be typical.

It is entrusted to the care of the Bishops' Conferences that the variants and additions made to the *Ordo Baptismi parvulorum* be inserted into the editions of the same *Ordo* appearing in the vernacular language.

All things to the contrary notwithstanding.

From the offices of the Sacred Congregation for Divine Worship, August 29, 1973, the Memorial of the Passion of Saint John the Baptist.

> ARTURO Cardinal TABERA
> Prefect

> ✠ A. BUGNINI
> Titular Archbishop of Diocletia
> Secretary

CONGREGATION FOR DIVINE WORSHIP
AND THE DISCIPLINE OF THE SACRAMENTS

Prot. n. 163/18

UNITED STATES OF AMERICA

At the request of His Eminence Daniel Cardinal DiNardo, Archbishop of Galveston-Houston, President of the Conference of Bishops of the United States of America, in a letter dated March 19, 2018, and by virtue of the faculty granted to this Congregation by the Supreme Pontiff FRANCIS, we gladly approve and confirm the text of the English translation, with recognized legitimate adaptations, of the part of the Roman Ritual entitled *Ordo Baptismi parvulorum, editio typica altera*, as found in the attached copy.

In printed editions, this decree must be inserted in its entirety.

Moreover, two copies of the printed text should be forwarded to this Congregation.

All things to the contrary notwithstanding.

From the offices of the Congregation for Divine Worship and the Discipline of the Sacraments, April 11, 2019, the Memorial of Saint Stanislaus, Bishop and Martyr.

ROBERT Card. SARAH
Prefect

✠ ARTHUR ROCHE
Archbishop Secretary

UNITED STATES CONFERENCE OF CATHOLIC BISHOPS

DECREE OF PUBLICATION

In accord with the norms established by the Holy See, this edition of the *Order of Baptism of Children* is declared to be the definitive approved English translation of the *Ordo Baptismi parvulorum, editio typica altera* (1973), and is published by authority of the United States Conference of Catholic Bishops.

The *Order of Baptism of Children* was canonically approved for use by the United States Conference of Catholic Bishops on November 14, 2017, and was subsequently confirmed by the Apostolic See by decree of the Congregation for Divine Worship and the Discipline of the Sacraments on April 11, 2019 (Prot. n. 163/18).

This rite may be used in the Liturgy as of February 2, 2020, the Feast of the Presentation of the Lord, and its use is obligatory as of April 12, 2020, Easter Sunday of the Resurrection of the Lord. From that date forward, no other English translation of the rite may be used in the dioceses of the United States of America.

Given at the General Secretariat of the United States Conference of Catholic Bishops, Washington, DC, on June 10, 2019, the Memorial of the Blessed Virgin Mary, Mother of the Church.

Daniel N. Cardinal DiNardo
Archbishop of Galveston-Houston
President, United States Conference of Catholic Bishops

Rev. Msgr. J. Brian Bransfield
General Secretary

CHRISTIAN INITIATION

GENERAL INTRODUCTION

1. Through the Sacraments of Christian Initiation all who have been freed from the power of darkness and have died, been buried and been raised with Christ, receive the Spirit of filial adoption and celebrate with the entire People of God the memorial of the Lord's Death and Resurrection.[1]

2. For, having been incorporated into Christ through Baptism, they are formed into the People of God, and, having received the remission of all their sins and been rescued from the power of darkness, they are brought to the status of adopted sons and daughters,[2] being made a new creation by water and the Holy Spirit. Hence they are called, and indeed are, children of God.[3] Sealed with the gift of the same Spirit in Confirmation, they are more perfectly configured to the Lord and filled with the Holy Spirit, so that bearing witness to Christ before the world, they bring the Body of Christ to its full stature without delay.[4] Finally, participating in the Eucharistic assembly (*synaxis*), they eat the Flesh and drink the Blood of the Son of Man, so that they may receive eternal life[5] and show forth the unity of God's people. Offering themselves with Christ, they take part in the universal sacrifice, which is the entire city of the redeemed offered to God through the great High Priest;[6] they also pray that, through a fuller outpouring of the Holy Spirit, the whole human race come into the unity of God's family.[7] Thus the three Sacraments of Christian Initiation so work together that they bring to full stature the Christian faithful, who exercise in the Church and in the world the mission of the entire Christian people.[8]

---

1. Second Vatican Council, Decree on the Church's Missionary Activity, *Ad gentes*, no. 14.

2. Cf. Colossians 1:13; Romans 8:15; Galatians 4:5. Cf. also Council of Trent, sess. 6., *Decr. de justificatione*, cap. 4: Denz.-Schön. 1524.

3. Cf. 1 John 3:1.

4. Cf. Second Vatican Council, Decree on the Church's Missionary Activity, *Ad gentes*, no. 36.

5. Cf. John 6:55.

6. Cf. Saint Augustine, *De civitate Dei* 10, 6: PL 41, 284. Vatican Council II, Dogmatic Constitution on the Church, *Lumen gentium*, no. 11; Decree on the Ministry and Life of Priests, *Presbyterorum ordinis*, no. 2.

7. Cf. Second Vatican Council, Dogmatic Constitution on the Church, *Lumen gentium*, no. 28.

8. Cf. *ibidem*, no. 31.

I. Dignity of Baptism

3. Baptism, the door to life and to the Kingdom, is the first Sacrament of the New Law, which Christ offered to all that they might have eternal life[9] and which, together with the Gospel, he later entrusted to his Church, when he commanded his Apostles: "Go, teach all nations, baptizing them in the name of the Father, and of the Son, and of the Holy Spirit."[10] Therefore Baptism is first and foremost the Sacrament of that faith by which human beings, enlightened by the grace of the Holy Spirit, respond to the Gospel of Christ. That is why the Church believes that there is nothing more ancient and nothing more proper for herself than to urge all—catechumens, parents of children who are to be baptized, and godparents—to that true and active faith by which, as they hold fast to Christ, they enter into or confirm the New Covenant. In fact, the pastoral instruction of catechumens and the preparation of parents, as well as the celebration of God's Word and the profession of baptismal faith, are all ordered to this end.

4. Furthermore, Baptism is the Sacrament by which human beings are incorporated into the Church and are built up together into a dwelling place of God in the Spirit,[11] and into a royal priesthood and a holy nation;[12] it is also a sacramental bond of unity linking all who are signed by it.[13] Because of that unchangeable effect (which the very celebration of the Sacrament in the Latin Liturgy makes clear when the baptized are anointed with Chrism, in the presence of the People of God), the rite of Baptism is held in highest honor by all Christians. Nor is it lawful for anyone to repeat it once it has been validly celebrated, even by separated brethren.

5. Moreover, the washing with water in the word of life,[14] which is what Baptism is, cleanses human beings of every stain of sin, both original and personal, and makes them sharers in the divine nature[15] and in filial adoption.[16] For Baptism, as is proclaimed in the prayers for the blessing of water, is the washing of regeneration[17] of the children of God and of birth from on high. The invocation of the Most Holy Trinity over those who are to be baptized has the effect that, signed with this name, they are consecrated to the Trinity and enter into fellowship with the Father, and the Son, and the Holy Spirit. This is the high point for

---

9. Cf. John 3:5.

10. Matthew 28:19.

11. Cf. Ephesians 2:22.

12. Cf. 1 Peter 2:9.

13. Cf. Second Vatican Council, Decree on Ecumenism, *Unitatis redintegratio*, no. 22.

14. Cf. Ephesians 5:26.

15. Cf. 2 Peter 1:4.

16. Cf. Romans 8:15; Galatians 4:5.

17. Cf. Titus 3:5.

which the biblical readings, the prayer of the community, and the threefold profession of faith prepare, and to which they lead.

6.   Baptism, far superior to the purifications of the Old Law, produces these effects by virtue of the mystery of the Lord's Passion and Resurrection. Those who are baptized are united with Christ in a death like his, are buried with him in death,[18] and also in him are given life and are raised up.[19] For in Baptism nothing other than the Paschal Mystery is recalled and accomplished, because in it human beings pass from the death of sin into life. Therefore, the joy of the resurrection should shine forth in the celebration of Baptism, especially when it takes place during the Easter Vigil or on a Sunday.

II. Duties and Ministries in the Celebration of Baptism

7.   Preparation for Baptism and Christian instruction are of the highest concern for the People of God, that is, for the Church, which hands on and nourishes the faith received from the Apostles. Through the ministry of the Church, adults are called to the Gospel by the Holy Spirit and infants are baptized and brought up in her faith. Therefore, it is very important that, in the preparation for Baptism, catechists and other laypersons should work with Priests and Deacons. Furthermore, in the celebration of Baptism, the People of God—represented not only by godparents, parents, and relatives, but also, insofar as possible, by friends, acquaintances, neighbors, and some members of the local Church—should take an active part, in order to show their common faith and to express their shared joy with which the newly baptized are received into the Church.

8.   In accordance with a most ancient custom of the Church, an adult is not admitted to Baptism without a godparent: a member of the Christian community who will already have assisted the candidate at least in the final preparation for receiving the Sacrament and who will help the candidate after Baptism to persevere in the faith and in the Christian life.

Likewise, at the Baptism of a child a godparent should be present in order to represent both the wider spiritual family of the one to be baptized and the role of the Church as mother and, as circumstances suggest, to help the parents so that the infant will come to profess the faith and to express it in life.

9.   At least in the later rites of the catechumenate and in the celebration of Baptism itself, the role of the godparent is to testify to the faith of the adult candidate or, together with the parents, to profess the Church's faith, in which the infant is baptized.

---

18. Cf. Romans 6:5, 4.

19. Cf. Ephesians 2:5–6.

10. Therefore the godparent, chosen by the catechumen or the family, must, in the judgment of the pastor of souls, be qualified to carry out the proper liturgical functions mentioned in no. 9, that is:

1. be designated by the one to be baptized or by the parents or by whoever takes their place or, in their absence, by the pastor or the minister of Baptism and have the aptitude and the intention to carry out this responsibility;
2. be mature enough to fulfill this responsibility; a person sixteen years old is presumed to have the requisite maturity, unless a different age has been established by the Diocesan Bishop or it seems to the pastor or minister that an exception is to be made for a just cause;
3. be initiated with the three Sacraments of Baptism, Confirmation, and Eucharist, and be living a life consistent with faith and the responsibility of a godparent;
4. be neither the father nor the mother of the one to be baptized;
5. be one godparent, male or female; but there may be two, one of each sex;
6. be a member of the Catholic Church, not prohibited by law from carrying out this office. A baptized person who belongs to a non-Catholic ecclesial community may be received only as a witness of the Baptism and only together with a Catholic godparent, at the request of the parents.[20] In the case of separated Eastern Christians, the special discipline for the Eastern Churches is to be respected.

11. The ordinary ministers of Baptism are Bishops, Priests, and Deacons.

1. In every celebration of this Sacrament they should be mindful that they act in the Church in the name of Christ and by the power of the Holy Spirit. They should therefore be diligent in the ministry of the Word of God and in the celebration of the Sacrament.
2. They should avoid any action that the faithful could rightly regard as favoritism.[21]
3. Except in a case of necessity, they are not to confer Baptism in the territory of another, even on their own subjects, without the required permission.

12. Bishops, who are indeed the chief stewards of the mysteries of God, just as they are also the moderators of the entire liturgical life in the Church entrusted to their care,[22] direct the conferring of Baptism, by which a participation in the royal priesthood of Christ is conferred.[23] They themselves should not neglect to

---

20. Cf. C.I.C., can. 873 and 874, § 1 and § 2.

21. Cf. Second Vatican Council, Constitution on the Sacred Liturgy, *Sacrosanctum Concilium*, no. 32; Pastoral Constitution on the Church in the Modern World, *Gaudium et spes*, no. 29.

22. Cf. Second Vatican Council, Decree on the Pastoral Office of Bishops, *Christus Dominus*, no. 15.

23. Cf. Second Vatican Council, Dogmatic Constitution on the Church, *Lumen gentium*, no. 26.

celebrate Baptism, especially at the Easter Vigil. The Baptism of adults and care for their preparation are especially entrusted to them.

13. It is the duty of pastors to assist the Bishop in the instruction and Baptism of the adults entrusted to their care, unless the Bishop makes other provisions. It is also their duty, with the assistance of catechists and other qualified laypersons, to prepare and assist the parents and godparents of children to be baptized through appropriate pastoral guidance, and finally to confer the Sacrament on infants.

14. Other Priests and Deacons, since they are co-workers in the ministry of Bishops and pastors, also prepare persons for Baptism, and confer it at the direction or with the consent of the Bishop or pastor.

15. The celebrant of Baptism may be assisted by other Priests or Deacons and also by laypersons in those parts that pertain to them, especially if there is a large number to be baptized, as is foreseen in respective parts of the ritual.

16. In imminent danger of death and especially at the moment of death, if no Priest or Deacon is present, any member of the faithful, indeed any person who has the requisite intention, can and sometimes must administer Baptism. But if there is only the danger of death, the Sacrament should be administered, if possible, by a member of the faithful and according to the shorter form (nos. 157–164). However, it is desirable that, even in this case, a small community should be gathered, or at least one or two witnesses should be present, if possible.

17. All laypersons, since they are members of the priestly people—but especially parents and, by reason of their work, catechists, midwives, women dedicated to works of social or family assistance or to the care of the sick, as well as physicians and surgeons—should take care to be thoroughly familiar, according to their capacities, with the correct method of baptizing in case of necessity. They should be taught by pastors, Deacons, and catechists, and Bishops should provide appropriate means for their instruction within the diocese.

III. Requisites for the Celebration of Baptism

18. Water used in Baptism should be natural and clean, so that the truth of the sign may be apparent, and also for hygienic reasons.

19. The font in the baptistery, or, as circumstances suggest, the vessel in which water is prepared for a celebration in the sanctuary, should be notable for its cleanliness and beauty.

20. Furthermore, provision should be made for the water to be warmed if the climate requires this.

21. Except in case of necessity, a Priest or Deacon is only to baptize with water that has been blessed for the purpose. If the consecration of water has taken place at the Easter Vigil, the blessed water should, insofar as possible, be kept and

used throughout Easter Time to signify more clearly the relationship between the Sacrament and the Paschal Mystery. However, outside Easter Time, it is desirable that the water be blessed for each celebration, so that the mystery of salvation that the Church remembers and proclaims may be clearly expressed in the words of consecration themselves. If the baptistery is constructed in such a way that the water flows, the source from which it flows should be blessed.

22.   Both the rite of immersion, which more suitably signifies participation in the Death and Resurrection of Christ, and the rite of pouring can lawfully be used.

23.   The words with which Baptism is conferred in the Latin Church are: *Ego te baptizo in nomine Patris, et Filii, et Spiritus Sancti* (*I baptize you in the name of the Father, and of the Son, and of the Holy Spirit*).

24.   A suitable place for celebrating the Word of God should be prepared in the baptistery or in the church.

25.   The baptistery (the place where the baptismal water flows or the font is located) should be reserved for the Sacrament of Baptism and be clearly worthy to serve as the place for Christians to be reborn of water and the Holy Spirit. Whether it is situated in a chapel inside or outside the church or in some other part of the church within the sight of the faithful, it must be organized so as to be suitable for the participation of a large number of people. After Easter Time, it is fitting for the paschal candle to be kept in a place of honor in the baptistery, so that, when it is lit for the celebration of Baptism, it is easy to light candles from it for the newly baptized.

26.   In celebrating Baptism, the rites that are to be performed outside the baptistery should take place in the different areas of the church that best suit both the number of those present and the various parts of the baptismal liturgy. It is also permitted to choose other suitable locations within the church for those parts that are normally celebrated inside the baptistery, if the chapel of the baptistery is unable to accommodate all the catechumens or all of those present.

27.   As far as possible, there should be a common celebration of Baptism on the same day for all newborn babies. Except for a just cause, Baptism should not be celebrated twice on the same day in the same church.

28.   More will be said concerning the time for Baptism of adults and of children in the appropriate places. But the celebration of the Sacrament should always have a markedly paschal character.

29.   Pastors must carefully and without delay record in the baptismal register the names of those baptized, of the minister, parents, and godparents, and of the place and date of the conferral of Baptism.

IV. Adaptations within the Competence of the Conferences of Bishops

30.   It is for Conferences of Bishops, by virtue of the Constitution on the Sacred Liturgy (no. 63b), to prepare for inclusion among their particular ritual books an edition corresponding to this one in the Roman Ritual, adapted to the needs of particular regions, so that, once their decisions have been accorded the *recognitio* of the Apostolic See, the edition may be used in the regions to which it pertains.

In this regard, it is for the Conferences of Bishops:

   1.   to determine the adaptations mentioned in no. 39 of the Constitution on the Sacred Liturgy;
   2.   to consider carefully and prudently what may appropriately be admitted from the traditions and culture of particular peoples, and consequently to propose to the Apostolic See other adaptations considered useful or necessary that are to be introduced with its consent;
   3.   to retain, or to adapt, distinctive elements of any existing local rituals, provided that they conform to the Constitution on the Sacred Liturgy and correspond to contemporary needs;
   4.   to prepare versions of the texts, so that they are truly adapted to the character of various languages and cultures, and to add, as appropriate, suitable melodies for singing;
   5.   to adapt and supplement the Introductions contained in the Roman Ritual, so that ministers may fully understand the meaning of the rites and perform them effectively;
   6.   in the various editions of the liturgical books to be prepared under the guidance of the Conferences of Bishops, to arrange the material in a form that seems most suitable for pastoral use.

31.   Taking into consideration especially the norms in the Constitution on the Sacred Liturgy, nos. 37–40 and 65, the Conferences of Bishops in mission countries have the responsibility to judge whether the elements of initiation in use among some peoples can be adapted for the rite of Christian Baptism and to decide whether such elements are to be incorporated into it.

32.   When the Roman Ritual for Baptism gives several optional formulas, local rituals may add other formulas of the same kind.

33.   Since the celebration of Baptism is greatly enhanced by singing—to stimulate a sense of unity among those present, to foster their common prayer, and to express the paschal joy with which the rite should resound—Conferences of Bishops should encourage and support skilled musicians to compose settings for those liturgical texts that are considered suitable to be sung by the faithful.

V. Adaptations within the Competence of the Minister

34.   Taking into account existing circumstances and other needs, as well as the wishes of the faithful, the minister should make generous use of the various options allowed in the rite.

35.   In addition to the optional formulas for the dialogue and blessings that are provided in the Roman Ritual itself, the minister may introduce certain adaptations for special circumstances, of which more will be said in the Introductions to Baptism for adults and for children.

THE ORDER OF BAPTISM OF CHILDREN

INTRODUCTION

I. IMPORTANCE OF THE BAPTISM OF CHILDREN

1.   The terms "children" or "infants" are to be understood as those who, since they have not yet reached the age of discretion, cannot profess the faith for themselves.

2.   From the first centuries, the Church, to whom the mission of evangelizing and baptizing has been given, baptized not only adults but also children. Since the Lord said, "No one can enter the Kingdom of God without being born of water and the Spirit,"[1] the Church has always understood that children are not to be deprived of Baptism, inasmuch as they are baptized in the faith of the Church herself, which is proclaimed by the parents and godparents and the others present. For they represent both the local Church and the whole company of Saints and faithful: Mother Church, who brings each and all to birth.[2]

3.   Furthermore, to bring to completion the reality of the Sacrament, children should afterwards be formed in the faith in which they have been baptized. The foundation of this formation will be the Sacrament itself which they have already received. Christian formation, which by right is owed to the children, has no other purpose than to lead them little by little to discern God's plan in Christ, so that ultimately they may be able to ratify the faith in which they have been baptized.

II. MINISTRIES AND DUTIES IN THE CELEBRATION OF BAPTISM

4.   The People of God, that is the Church represented by the local community, plays just as important a part in the Baptism of children as in that of adults.
    For a child, both before and after the celebration of the Sacrament, has the right to the love and help of the community. Moreover, during the rite, besides those things listed as pertaining to the gathered assembly in no. 7 of *Christian Initiation*, General Introduction, the community exercises its function when, together with the celebrant, it expresses its consent after the profession of faith

---

1. John 3:5.
2. Saint Augustine, Epistle 98, 5: PL 33, 362.

by the parents and godparents. In this way, it becomes apparent that the faith in which the children are being baptized is a treasure not belonging to the family alone, but to the whole Church of Christ.

5.   From the order of creation itself, the ministry and duty of parents in the Baptism of children carry greater weight than the duty of godparents.

    1.   Before the celebration of the Sacrament it is very helpful for the parents, either led by their own faith, or aided by the support of their friends or of other members of the community, to prepare themselves for an informed participation in the celebration by suitable means, such as books, articles, and catechisms aimed at the family. Furthermore, the pastor of the parish should take care to meet with them himself or through others, or even to bring together several families, to prepare them for the coming celebration by pastoral instructions and prayer in common.

    2.   It is of great importance for the parents of the child being baptized to be present at the celebration in which their child will be reborn of water and the Holy Spirit.

    3.   The parents of the child carry out the parts truly proper to them in the celebration of Baptism. Besides the instructions of the celebrant which they hear and the prayer which they make with the whole company of the faithful, they perform a true ministry when: a) they ask publicly that the child be baptized; b) they sign the child on the forehead after the celebrant; c) they renounce Satan and make the profession of faith; d) they (the mother in particular) carry the infant to the font; e) they hold the lighted candle; f) they are blessed with the formulas especially intended for mothers and fathers.

    4.   If one of them is not able to make the profession of faith, for example, because one of the parents is not a Catholic, that parent may remain silent. Given that the Baptism of the child has been requested, the only requirement is that he or she provide for or at least permit the instruction of the child in the baptismal faith.

    5.   After the conferral of Baptism, the parents, grateful to God and faithful to the duty they have undertaken, are bound to guide their child to a knowledge of God, now his child by adoption. They are also bound to prepare the child to receive Confirmation and to participate in the Most Holy Eucharist. In this duty they are again to be helped in suitable ways by the pastor of the parish.

6.   Each child may have a godfather and a godmother. In the Order of the rite itself both are indicated by the name "godparent."

7.   In addition to what is said in *Christian Initiation*, General Introduction about the ordinary minister (nos. 11–15), the following points should be noted:

1. It is for pastors to prepare families for the Baptism of their children and to help them fulfill the responsibility of formation, which they have now undertaken. Furthermore, it is for the Bishop to coordinate such pastoral initiatives in his diocese, with the help also of Deacons and laypeople.

2. It is for pastors also to make every effort that each Baptism be celebrated with due dignity and that it be accommodated, as far as possible, to the circumstances and wishes of the families. Whoever is conferring Baptism should carry out the rite carefully and reverently; he should strive above all to be courteous and affable to everyone.

III. Time and Place for the Baptism of Children

8.   With regard to the time for the conferral of Baptism, the first consideration should be the welfare of the child, lest he or she be deprived of the benefit of the Sacrament. The next consideration should be the health of the mother, so that, as far as possible, she may also be present. So long as it does not conflict with the greater good of the child, the final consideration should be the pastoral need to allow sufficient time to prepare the parents and properly to arrange the celebration itself, so that the nature of the rite may be evident.

Therefore:

1. A child in danger of death is to be baptized without delay. This is permitted even against the will of the parents, even if the parents of the infant are non-Catholics. Baptism is then conferred in the manner specified below (no. 21).

2. In other cases, the parents, at least one of them or the person who legitimately takes their place, must consent to the Baptism. In order to prepare properly for the celebration of the Sacrament, they should contact the pastor of the parish as soon as possible about the future Baptism, even before the birth of the child, if circumstances suggest.

3. The celebration of Baptism should take place during the first weeks after the birth of the child. If there is no hope whatever that the child will be brought up in the Catholic religion, the Baptism is to be delayed according to the prescripts of particular law (cf. no. 25), after the parents have been advised of the reason.

4. It is for the pastor of the parish, when the conditions above do not apply, to decide the times for the Baptism of children, keeping in mind any regulations laid down by the Conference of Bishops.

9.   To illustrate the paschal character of Baptism, it is recommended that the Sacrament be celebrated at the Easter Vigil or on a Sunday, when the Church commemorates the Resurrection of the Lord. Furthermore, on a Sunday, Baptism may be celebrated also within Mass, so that the whole community may be able to

take part in the rite and so that the connection between Baptism and the Most Holy Eucharist may stand out more clearly. Nevertheless, this should not happen too often. Other norms for the celebration of Baptism at the Easter Vigil or during the Sunday Mass will be set out below.

10. In order that Baptism may be seen more clearly as the Sacrament of the Church's faith and of incorporation into the People of God, it should normally be celebrated in the parish church, which ought to have a baptismal font.

11. Moreover, it is for the Ordinary of the place, having consulted the pastor of the parish, to permit or order that a baptismal font be placed in another church or oratory within the boundaries of the parish. But even in these places, the pastor of the parish should normally celebrate Baptism.

But when, because of distance or other circumstances, the one to be baptized cannot go or be brought to the place without great difficulty, Baptism can and must be conferred in another nearer church or oratory, or even in another suitable place, with due regard for what is laid down for the time and structure of the celebration (cf. nos. 8–9, 15–22).

12. Apart from a case of necessity, Baptism is not to be celebrated in private houses, unless for a grave reason the Ordinary of the place has permitted it.

13. Unless the Bishop has established otherwise (cf. no. 11), Baptism is not to be celebrated in hospitals, except in a case of necessity or for some other compelling pastoral reason. But care should always be taken that the pastor of the parish be informed, and suitable preparation be given to the parents.

14. While the Liturgy of the Word is celebrated, it is desirable that children should be taken to a separate place. But care should be taken that the parents and godparents attend the Liturgy of the Word; the children should therefore be entrusted to the care of others.

IV. STRUCTURE OF THE RITE OF BAPTIZING CHILDREN

A. Order of Baptism to Be Celebrated by an Ordinary Minister

15. Whether there is one child, or several, or many to be baptized, if there is no immediate danger of death, the celebrant should follow the entire rite, as described here.

16. The rite begins with the reception of the children, in which are signified the desire of the parents and godparents and the intention of the Church regarding the celebration of the Sacrament of Baptism. These intentions are expressed by the parents and celebrant by signing the children on the forehead.

17. The sacred celebration of the Word of God is intended to stir up the faith of the parents and godparents and others present, and to encourage them to pray together for the fruits of the Sacrament, before the sacramental action. This

celebration of the Liturgy of the Word consists of the reading of one or more passages of Sacred Scripture; a homily, followed by a period of silence; the Prayer of the Faithful, and the concluding prayer, drawn up in the form of an exorcism, which introduces the anointing with the Oil of Catechumens or, if there is no anointing, the laying on of hands.

18.   Furthermore, the celebration of the Sacrament

    1.   has as its immediate preparation:
        a) both the solemn prayer of the celebrant which, by invoking God and recalling his plan of salvation, either blesses the water of Baptism or commemorates its blessing;
        b) and the renunciation of Satan and the profession of faith by the parents and godparents, to which is added the assent of the celebrant and community, and the final questioning of the parents and godparents;
    2.   is performed by washing in water, which may be done by immersion or by pouring, according to the custom of the place, and by the invocation of the Most Holy Trinity;
    3.   is completed, first by the anointing with Chrism, by which is signified the royal priesthood of the baptized and enrollment into the company of the People of God; then by the rites of the white garment, the lighted candle and the "Ephphatha" (the last of which is optional).

19.   After the celebrant's instruction, to anticipate the future sharing in the Eucharist, the Lord's Prayer, in which the children of God pray to their Father in heaven, is said before the altar. Then, so that the grace of God may be poured out on all, the mothers and fathers, and all present, are blessed.

B. Shorter Order of Baptism

20.   In the shorter Order of Baptism for the use of catechists[3] the rite of reception of the children, the celebration of the Word of God, or the instruction of the minister, and the Prayer of the Faithful, take place. Before the font, the minister offers a prayer invoking God and recalling the history of salvation with respect to Baptism. After the baptismal washing, the anointing with Chrism is omitted and the adapted formula is recited instead. The whole rite is completed with the usual conclusion. Thus the exorcism, the anointing with the Oil of Catechumens, the anointing with Chrism, and the "Ephphatha" are omitted.

21.   The shorter Order for baptizing children in danger of death, in the absence of the ordinary minister, has a twofold structure:

    1.   At the point of death or, when death is imminent and time is pressing, the minister,[4] omitting everything else, pours water (not necessarily

---

3. Cf. Second Vatican Council, Constitution on the Sacred Liturgy, *Sacrosanctum Concilium*, no. 68.

4. Cf. *Christian Initiation*, General Introduction, no. 16.

blessed, but natural water) over the head of the child, reciting the customary formula.[5]

2. But if it is prudently judged that there is sufficient time, several of the faithful may be gathered, and if one of them is capable of leading a brief prayer, the following rite should be used: an explanation by the minister and a short prayer of the faithful, a profession of faith by the parents or by one godparent, and the pouring of water with the appropriate words, take place. But if those present are not well educated, the minister, after reciting the Creed aloud, baptizes the child according to the rite to be followed at the point of death.

22.   A Priest or Deacon may also use the shorter Order, if necessary, in imminent danger of death. Moreover, the pastor of the parish or other Priest possessing the same faculty, if he has the sacred Chrism at hand and time permits, should not fail to administer Confirmation after the Baptism. In this case the post-baptismal anointing with Chrism is omitted.

V. ADAPTATIONS WHICH CONFERENCES OF BISHOPS OR BISHOPS MAY MAKE

23.   Besides the adaptations provided for in *Christian Initiation*, General Introduction (nos. 30–33), the rites for baptizing children allow for other variations to be determined by Conferences of Bishops.

24.   In the Dioceses of the United States of America:

1. According to the customs of the place, the questioning about the name of the child to be baptized may be arranged in various ways: the name may have been given already, or may be given in the act of Baptism.
2. The anointing with the Oil of Catechumens may be omitted only when the minister of Baptism judges the omission to be pastorally necessary or desirable (nos. 50, 87).
3. The norm is that the formula of renunciation should not be adapted. However, the second formula of renunciation may be made more pointed and detailed at the discretion of the Diocesan Bishop, especially when it is necessary that the parents and godparents should renounce superstitions, divinations, and magical arts practiced with reference to the children (nos. 57, 94, 121).
4. Even if very many children are to be baptized, the anointing with Chrism is not to be omitted (no. 125).
5. The "Ephphatha" rite may be retained at the discretion of the minister of Baptism (nos. 65, 101).

---

5. Cf. *ibidem*, no. 23.

---

25. Since in many regions parents may not yet be ready for the celebration of Baptism, or they may ask that their children be baptized, even though they will not afterwards be brought up as Christians, and may even lose their faith, it is not sufficient that the parents be instructed in their faith and questioned about it in the rite itself. Conferences of Bishops, to help pastors of parishes, may issue pastoral directives, to determine a longer interval of time before the celebration of the Sacrament.

26. It especially belongs to the Bishop to decide for his diocese whether the catechists may freely deliver an instruction in their own words after the biblical readings or read a written text.

VI. Adaptations within the Competence of the Minister

27. During the meetings at which the parents are prepared for the Baptism of their children, it is of great importance that the instructions be supported by prayers and the rites. For this purpose it may help to use the various elements that are provided in the Order of Baptism for the celebration of the Word of God.

28. When the Baptism of children is celebrated during the Easter Vigil, the service is arranged as follows:

1. Before the celebration of the Easter Vigil, at a convenient time and place, the rite of receiving the children is carried out. At the end of this, if appropriate, the Liturgy of the Word is omitted, and the prayer of exorcism and the anointing with the Oil of Catechumens take place.

2. The celebration of the Sacrament itself (nos. 56–58, 60–63) takes place after the blessing of water, as indicated in the Order of the Easter Vigil itself.

3. The assent of the celebrant and community is omitted (no. 59), as is the handing on of the lighted candle (no. 64) and the "Ephphatha" rite (no. 65).

4. The conclusion of the rite is omitted (nos. 67–71).

29. When Baptism is conferred during Sunday Mass, the Mass of the day is said or, during the Sundays of Christmas Time or of Ordinary Time, the Mass for the Conferral of Baptism is said. The celebration is arranged as follows:

1. The rite of receiving the child (nos. 33–43; cf. nos. 257–265, 296–303) is done at the beginning of the Mass, and the Greeting and Penitential Act are omitted.

2. In the Liturgy of the Word:
   a) The readings are taken from the Mass of the Sunday. During Christmas Time and Ordinary Time they may also be taken from those which are given in the *Lectionary for Mass* (nos. 756–760) or in this Order (nos. 44, 186–215; cf. nos. 269, 307).

When a Ritual Mass is not permitted, one of the readings may be taken from the texts provided for the Baptism of children, having due regard for the pastoral needs of the faithful and the character of the liturgical day.

b) The Homily is based on the sacred text, but should take into consideration the Baptism being celebrated.

c) The Creed is not said, because its place is taken by the profession of faith, which is made by the entire community before the Baptism.

d) The Universal Prayer (Prayer of the Faithful) is taken from those in the *Order of Baptism* (nos. 47–48, 217–220; cf. nos. 272–273, 310–311). At the end, however, before the invocation of the Saints, petitions are added for the universal Church and for the needs of the world.

3. The celebration of Baptism continues with the prayer of exorcism and the anointing and the other rites described in the *Order of Baptism* (nos. 49–66; cf. nos. 274–291, 312–327).

4. When the celebration of Baptism is concluded, the Mass continues as usual with the Offertory.

5. For imparting the blessing at the end of Mass, the Priest may use one of the formulas which are given for the rite of Baptism (nos. 70, 247–249; cf. nos. 293, 329).

30. On weekdays, if Baptism is celebrated within Mass, the order is for the most part the same as on a Sunday; but in the Liturgy of the Word the readings may be taken from those given for the rite of Baptism (nos. 44, 186–215; cf. nos. 269, 307).

31. In accordance with what is said in no. 34 of *Christian Initiation*, General Introduction, the minister may make some adaptations in the rite, as the circumstances require, such as:

1. if the mother of the child died in childbirth, this should be taken into account in the opening instruction (no. 36), in the Universal Prayer or Prayer of the Faithful (nos. 47, 217–220) and in the final blessing (nos. 70, 247–248);

2. in the dialogue with the parents (nos. 37–38, 76–77), notice should be taken of their replies. If they have not said "Baptism" but "Faith" or "The grace of Christ" or "Entry into the Church" or "Eternal life," the minister should not begin with the words "In asking for Baptism for your children" but appropriately with: "Faith" or "The grace of Christ," etc.;

3. the Order of Bringing an Already-Baptized Child into the Church (nos. 165–185), which has been drawn up for the sole case of a child baptized in danger of death, may be adapted to other needs, e.g., if children have been baptized in time of religious persecution or temporary disagreement between the parents.

N.B. The liturgical texts which refer to males may be adapted to females, changing the gender; or to several people, changing the number.

CHAPTER I
ORDER OF BAPTISM FOR SEVERAL CHILDREN

RITE OF RECEIVING THE CHILDREN

32.   Baptism should be celebrated, insofar as possible, on a Sunday, the day on which the Church recalls the Paschal Mystery, and indeed in a common celebration for all the newly born, and with the attendance of a large number of the faithful, or at least of the relatives, friends, and neighbors, and with their active participation.

33.   It is for the father and mother, together with the godparents, to present the child to the Church for Baptism.

34.   If there are very many children to be baptized, and there are several Priests or Deacons present, these may assist the celebrant in performing those rites that are indicated in the text.

35.   The faithful sing a suitable Psalm or hymn, if circumstances allow. Meanwhile, the Priest or Deacon celebrant, wearing an alb or surplice and stole, and even a cope, in a festive color, goes with the ministers to the door of the church, or to that part of the church where the parents and godparents are gathered with those to be baptized.

36.   The celebrant greets those present, especially the parents and godparents, recalling in a few words the joy with which the parents received their children as a gift from God, who is the source of all life and who now wishes to bestow his own life on them. He may use these or similar words:

Dear parents and godparents:
Your families have experienced great joy at the birth
      of your children,
and the Church shares your happiness.
Today this joy has brought you to the Church
to give thanks to God for the gift of your children
and to celebrate a new birth in the waters of Baptism.

This community rejoices with you,
for today the number of those baptized in Christ will be increased,
and we offer you our support in raising your children
in the practice of the faith.
Therefore, brothers and sisters,
let us now prepare ourselves to participate in this celebration,
listening to God's Word, praying for these children
        and their families,
and renewing our commitment to the Lord and to his people.

37.   The celebrant first asks the parents of each child:

What name do you give (or: have you given) your child?

Parents:

N.

Celebrant:

What do you ask of God's Church for N.?

Parents:

Baptism.

The celebrant may use other words in this dialogue.

The first reply may be given by another person if, according to local custom, this person has the right to give the name.

In the second reply, the parents may use other words: e.g., Faith or The grace of Christ or Entry into the Church or Eternal life.

38. If there are many to be baptized, the celebrant may ask all the parents at once for the names of their children:

What name do you give (or: have you given) your child?

Each family replies in turn. The second question may be put to all at once in the plural.

Celebrant:

What do you ask of God's Church for your children?

All:

Baptism.

39. Then the celebrant addresses the parents in these or similar words:

In asking for Baptism for your children,
you are undertaking the responsibility
of raising them in the faith,
so that, keeping God's commandments,
they may love the Lord and their neighbor as Christ has taught us.
Do you understand this responsibility?

Parents:

We do.

This reply is given by each family individually; but if the number of children to be baptized is very large, the reply may be given by all together.

40. Then turning to the godparents, the celebrant asks in these or similar words:

Are you ready to help the parents of these children in their duty?

All the godparents together:

We are.

41.   Then the celebrant continues, saying:

N. and N. (or: **Dear children**),
the Church of God receives you with great joy.
In her name I sign you with the Sign of the Cross
 of Christ our Savior;
then, after me, your parents (and godparents) will do the same.

> And, without saying anything, he signs each of the children on the
> forehead. Afterwards he invites the parents, and if it seems appropri-
> ate, the godparents, to do the same.

> 42.   The celebrant invites the parents, godparents, and others present
> to take part in the celebration of the Word of God. If circumstances
> permit, a procession to the appointed place takes place with singing
> (e.g., Psalm 85 [84]:7–9ab).

> Psalm 85 (84):7–9ab

Will you not restore again our life,
 that your people may rejoice in you?
Show us, O Lord, your mercy,
 and grant us your salvation.
I will hear what the Lord God speaks;
 he speaks of peace for his people and his faithful.

> 43.   The children to be baptized may be taken to a separate place,
> until the celebration of the Word of God is completed.

Sacred Celebration of the Word of God

Biblical Readings and Homily

> 44.   If it seems appropriate, one, or even two, of the following passages
> is read, while all are seated.
>
> Mt 28:18–20: *Go, therefore, and make disciples of all nations, baptizing
> them in the name of the Father, and of the Son, and of the Holy Spirit* (no.
> 205).
>
> Mk 1:9–11: *Jesus was baptized in the Jordan by John* (no. 206).
>
> Mk 10:13–16: *Let the children come to me; do not prevent them* (no. 207).

Jn 3:1–6: *No one can see the Kingdom of God without being born from above* (no. 209).

The passages that are to be found at nos. 186–194 and 204–215, or others suited to the wishes or needs of the parents, may also be chosen.

Between the Readings, the Responsorial Psalms or the Verses provided in nos. 195–203 may be sung.

45.   After the Reading, the celebrant preaches a brief homily in which light is shed on what has been read, and those present are led to a deeper understanding of the mystery of Baptism and to a more eager fulfillment of the responsibility that arises from it, especially for parents and godparents.

46.   After the Homily, or after the Litany, or even during the Litany, it is recommended that there be a period of silence in which all, invited by the celebrant, pray in their hearts. There follows, if the situation warrants, a suitable liturgical song, chosen, for example, from among those provided in nos. 225–245.

Prayer of the Faithful

47.   Then the Prayer of the Faithful takes place.

Celebrant:

Dear brothers and sisters,
let us invoke the mercy of our Lord Jesus Christ
for these children about to receive the grace of Baptism,
and for their parents, godparents, and all the baptized.

Lector:

Give these children new birth in Baptism
through the radiant divine mystery of your Death and Resurrection,
and join them to your holy Church:

All:

Lord, we ask you, hear our prayer.

Lector:

Make them faithful disciples and witnesses to your Gospel through Baptism and Confirmation:

All:

Lord, we ask you, hear our prayer.

Lector:

Lead them through holiness of life to the joys of the heavenly Kingdom:

All:

Lord, we ask you, hear our prayer.

Lector:

Make their parents and godparents a shining example of the faith to these children:

All:

Lord, we ask you, hear our prayer.

Lector:

Keep their families always in your love:

All:

Lord, we ask you, hear our prayer.

Lector:

Renew the grace of Baptism in each of us:

All:

Lord, we ask you, hear our prayer.

Other optional formulas, nos. 217–220.

48.   Afterwards, the celebrant invites those present to invoke the aid of the Saints (if the circumstances require, the children are brought back into the church):

Holy Mary, Mother of God,   pray for us.
Saint John the Baptist,   pray for us.
Saint Joseph,   pray for us.
Saint Peter and Saint Paul,

It is good to add the nam(*Extend over*
Patron Saints of the chil(
the Litany concludes:

All holy men and women, !

Optional extended form o   *Anoint OC after*
Low Hands

PRAYER OF EXORCISM AND ANOINTING BEFORE BAPTISM

49.   After the invocations, the celebrant says:

Almighty ever-living God,
who sent your Son into the world
to drive out from us the power of Satan, the spirit of evil,
and bring the human race, rescued from darkness,
into the marvelous Kingdom of your light:
we humbly beseech you
to free these children from Original Sin,
to make them the temple of your glory,
and to grant that your Holy Spirit may dwell in them.
Through Christ our Lord.

All:

Amen.

Another formula for the Prayer of Exorcism, no. 221.

50.   The celebrant continues:

May the strength of Christ the Savior protect you.
As a sign of this we anoint you with the oil of salvation
in the same Christ our Lord,
who lives and reigns for ever and ever.

All:

Amen.

> Those to be baptized are anointed one at a time on the breast with the Oil of Catechumens. If there are many children, it is permitted to make use of several ministers.

> 51.   In the United States, if, for serious reasons, the celebrant judges it pastorally necessary or desirable, the Anointing before Baptism may be omitted. In that case, the celebrant says only once:

May the strength of Christ the Savior protect you;
who lives and reigns for ever and ever.

All:

Amen.

> And immediately, without saying anything, he lays his hand on each of the children.

> 52.   Then, if the baptistery is outside the church or out of sight of the faithful, there is a procession to it.

> But if it is located within view of the congregation, the celebrant, parents, and godparents go there with the children and the others remain in their places.

> If the baptistery cannot accommodate all those present, it is permitted to celebrate the Baptism in a more suitable place, with the parents and godparents coming forward at the appropriate time.

> Meanwhile, if it can be done with dignity, a suitable liturgical song is sung, e.g., Psalm 23 (22).

> Psalm 23 (22)

The LORD is my shepherd;
      there is nothing I shall want.
Fresh and green are the pastures
      where he gives me repose.
Near restful waters he leads me;
      he revives my soul.

He guides me along the right path,
 for the sake of his name.
Though I should walk in the valley of the shadow of death,
 no evil would I fear, for you are with me.
Your crook and your staff will give me comfort.

You have prepared a table before me
 in the sight of my foes.
My head you have anointed with oil;
 my cup is overflowing.

Surely goodness and mercy shall follow me
 all the days of my life.
In the Lord's own house shall I dwell
 for length of days unending.

Celebration of Baptism

53. When they have come to the font, the celebrant briefly reminds those present of the wonderful plan of God, who willed to sanctify the human soul and body through water. He may do this in these or similar words:

**Let us pray, dear brothers and sisters,
that the Lord God Almighty may bestow new life on these children
by water and the Holy Spirit.**

Or:

**Dear brothers and sisters,
you know that God graciously bestows
his abundant life through the sacrament of water
on those who believe.
Let us then raise our minds to him,
and with one heart pray
that he may be pleased to pour out his grace from this font
upon these chosen ones.**

54. Then, turning to the font, the celebrant says the following Blessing (outside Easter Time):

O God, who by invisible power
accomplish a wondrous effect
through sacramental signs
and who in many ways have prepared water, your creation,
to show forth the grace of Baptism;

O God, whose Spirit
in the first moments of the world's creation
hovered over the waters,
so that the very substance of water
would even then take to itself the power to sanctify;

O God, who by the outpouring of the flood
foreshadowed regeneration,
so that from the mystery of one and the same element of water
would come an end to vice and a beginning of virtue;

O God, who caused the children of Abraham
to pass dry-shod through the Red Sea,
so that the chosen people,
set free from slavery to Pharaoh,
would prefigure the people of the baptized;

O God, whose Son,
baptized by John in the waters of the Jordan,
was anointed with the Holy Spirit,
and, as he hung upon the Cross,
gave forth water from his side along with blood,
and after his Resurrection, commanded his disciples:
"Go forth, teach all nations, baptizing them
in the name of the Father and of the Son and of the Holy Spirit,"
look now, we pray, upon the face of your Church
and graciously unseal for her the fountain of Baptism.

May this water receive by the Holy Spirit
the grace of your Only Begotten Son,
so that human nature, created in your image
and washed clean through the Sacrament of Baptism
from all the squalor of the life of old,
may be found worthy to rise to the life of newborn children
through water and the Holy Spirit.

The celebrant touches the water with his right hand and continues:

May the power of the Holy Spirit,
O Lord, we pray,
come down through your Son
into the fullness of this font,
so that all who have been buried with Christ
by Baptism into death
may rise again to life with him.
Who lives and reigns for ever and ever.

All:

Amen.

Other optional formulas, nos. 223–224.

55.   During Easter Time, however, if the baptismal water has been consecrated at the Easter Vigil, so that the Baptism may not lack the element of thanksgiving and petition, the blessing and invocation of God over the water takes place in accordance with the formulas found in nos. 223–224, using the textual variation given at the end of these same formulas.

RENUNCIATION OF SIN AND PROFESSION OF FAITH

56.   The celebrant instructs the parents and godparents in these words:

Dear parents and godparents:
through the Sacrament of Baptism
the children you have presented
are about to receive from the love of God
new life by water and the Holy Spirit.

For your part, you must strive to bring them up in the faith,
so that this divine life may be preserved from the contagion of sin,
and may grow in them day by day.

If your faith makes you ready to accept this responsibility,
then, mindful of your own Baptism,
renounce sin and profess faith in Christ Jesus,
the faith of the Church,
in which children are baptized.

57.   Then the celebrant questions them:

Do you renounce Satan?

Parents and godparents:

I do.

Celebrant:

And all his works?

Parents and godparents:

I do.

Celebrant:

And all his empty show?

Parents and godparents:

I do.

Or:

Celebrant:

**Do you renounce sin,
so as to live in the freedom of the children of God?**

Parents and godparents:

I do.

Celebrant:

**Do you renounce the lure of evil,
so that sin may have no mastery over you?**

Parents and godparents:

I do.

Celebrant:

**Do you renounce Satan,
the author and prince of sin?**

Parents and godparents:

I do.

In the United States, if the occasion requires, this second formula may be adapted with more precision by the Diocesan Bishop, especially when it is necessary that the parents and godparents should renounce superstitions, divinations, and magical arts practiced with reference to the children.

58.   Next, the celebrant elicits the threefold profession of faith by the parents and godparents, saying:

**Do you believe in God,
the Father almighty,
Creator of heaven and earth?**

Parents and godparents:

I do.

Celebrant:

**Do you believe in Jesus Christ, his only Son, our Lord,
who was born of the Virgin Mary,
suffered death and was buried,
rose again from the dead
and is seated at the right hand of the Father?**

Parents and godparents:

I do.

Celebrant:

Do you believe in the Holy Spirit,
the holy catholic Church,
the communion of saints,
the forgiveness of sins,
the resurrection of the body,
and life everlasting?

Parents and godparents:

I do.

59.   The celebrant, together with the community, gives assent to this profession of faith, saying:

This is our faith. This is the faith of the Church.
We are proud to profess it in Christ Jesus our Lord.

All:

Amen.

Another formula may be substituted, if circumstances suggest. Or a suitable liturgical song, by which the community expresses its faith with one voice, may be sung.

Baptism

60.   The celebrant invites the first family to approach the font. In addition, using the name of the individual child, he asks the parents and godparents:

Is it your will, therefore, that N. should receive Baptism in the faith
of the Church, which we have all professed with you?

Parents and godparents:

It is.

And immediately the celebrant baptizes the child, saying:

N., I BAPTIZE YOU IN THE NAME OF THE FATHER,

He immerses the child or pours water over him (her) a first time.

AND OF THE SON,

He immerses the child or pours water over him (her) a second time.

AND OF THE HOLY SPIRIT.

He immerses the child or pours water over him (her) a third time.

He asks the same question and does the same for each child to be baptized.

After the Baptism of each child, it is appropriate for the people to sing a short acclamation, such as:

Blessed be God, who chose you in Christ.

Other optional acclamations, nos. 225–245.

If the Baptism is celebrated by the pouring of water, it is preferable for the child to be held by the mother (or by the father); however, where it is felt that the existing custom should be retained, the child may be held by the godmother (or by the godfather). If the Baptism is by immersion, the child is lifted from the sacred font by the same person.

61.   If there are many children to be baptized, and there are several Priests or Deacons present, each of them may baptize some of the children, by using the same method and formula described above.

Explanatory Rites

Anointing after Baptism

62. Then the celebrant says:

Almighty God, the Father of our Lord Jesus Christ,
has freed you from sin,
given you new birth by water and the Holy Spirit,
and joined you to his people.
He now anoints you with the Chrism of salvation,
so that you may remain members of Christ,
    Priest, Prophet and King,
unto eternal life.

All:

Amen.

Then, without saying anything, the celebrant anoints each baptized child with sacred Chrism on the crown of his (her) head.

If there are a large number of baptized children and there are several Priests or Deacons present, each of them may anoint some of the children with Chrism.

Clothing with a White Garment

63. The celebrant says:

(N. and N.,) you have become a new creation
and have clothed yourselves in Christ.
May this white garment be a sign to you of your Christian dignity.
With your family and friends to help you by word and example,
bring it unstained into eternal life.

All:

Amen.

And a white garment is placed on each child; another color is not permitted, unless it is demanded by local custom. It is desirable that the families themselves provide this garment.

Handing On of a Lighted Candle

64.   The celebrant then takes the paschal candle and says:

Receive the light of Christ.

One member of each family (e.g., the father or godfather) lights a candle for each child from the paschal candle.

Then the celebrant says:

Parents and godparents,
this light is entrusted to you to be kept burning brightly,
so that your children, enlightened by Christ,
may walk always as children of the light
and, persevering in the faith,
may run to meet the Lord when he comes
with all the Saints in the heavenly court.

"Ephphatha"

65.   In the United States, the "Ephphatha" Rite takes place at the discretion of the celebrant. The celebrant touches the ears and mouth of each child with his thumb, saying:

May the Lord Jesus,
who made the deaf to hear and the mute to speak,
grant that you may soon receive his word with your ears
and profess the faith with your lips,
to the glory and praise of God the Father.

All:

Amen.

66.   If there are many children, the celebrant says the formula once, omitting the touching of the ears and mouth.

Conclusion of the Rite

67.   Afterwards, unless the Baptism took place in the sanctuary, there is a procession to the altar, in which the lighted candles of the newly baptized are carried.

Meanwhile, it is desirable that a baptismal canticle be sung, e.g.:

Baptized in Christ,
you are clothed with Christ,
alleluia, alleluia.

Other optional canticles, nos. 225–245.

Lord's Prayer

68.   The celebrant, standing before the altar, addresses the parents and godparents and all present in these or similar words:

Dear brothers and sisters:
these children, reborn through Baptism,
are now called children of God, for so indeed they are.

Through Confirmation they will receive the fullness
        of the Holy Spirit
and, approaching the altar of the Lord,
they will share at the table of his Sacrifice,
and will call upon God as Father in the midst of the Church.
Now in their name,
and in the spirit of adoption as sons and daughters
which we have all received,
let us pray together as the Lord taught us.

69.   And all say together with the celebrant:

Our Father, who art in heaven,
hallowed be thy name;
thy kingdom come,
thy will be done
on earth as it is in heaven.

Give us this day our daily bread,
and forgive us our trespasses,
as we forgive those who trespass against us;
and lead us not into temptation,
but deliver us from evil.

Blessing and Dismissal

70. Then the celebrant blesses the mothers, holding their children in their arms, the fathers, and all those present, saying:

The Lord God Almighty,
through his Son, born of the Virgin Mary,
brings joy to Christian mothers
as the hope of eternal life shines forth upon their children.
May he graciously bless the mothers of these children,
so that, as they now give thanks for the gift of their children,
they may always remain united with them in thanksgiving,
in Christ Jesus our Lord.

All:

Amen.

Celebrant:

May the Lord God Almighty,
the giver of life both in heaven and on earth,
bless the fathers of these children,
so that, together with their wives,
they may, by word and example,
prove to be the first witnesses of the faith to their children,
in Christ Jesus our Lord.

All:

Amen.

Celebrant:

May the Lord God Almighty,
who by water and the Holy Spirit
has given us new birth into eternal life,
abundantly bless his faithful here present,
that always and everywhere they may be active members
    of his people;
and may he bestow his peace on all who are here,
in Christ Jesus our Lord.

All:

Amen.

Celebrant:

May almighty God bless you,
the Father, and the Son, ✝ and the Holy Spirit.

All:

Amen.

Celebrant:

Go in peace.

All:

Thanks be to God.

Other optional formulas of blessing, nos. 247–249.

71.   After the blessing, if circumstances suggest, a suitable canticle that expresses paschal joy and thanksgiving or the Canticle of the Blessed Virgin Mary, the **Magnificat**, may be sung by all.

Where it is the custom to bring the baptized infants to the altar of the Blessed Virgin Mary, this custom should appropriately be retained.

Chapter II
ORDER OF BAPTISM FOR ONE CHILD

Rite of Receiving the Child

72. Baptism should be celebrated, insofar as possible, on a Sunday, the day on which the Church recalls the Paschal Mystery, with the attendance of a large number of the faithful, or at least of the relatives, friends, and neighbors, and with their active participation.

73. It is for the father and mother, together with the godparents, to present the child to the Church for Baptism.

74. The faithful sing a suitable Psalm or hymn, if circumstances allow. Meanwhile, the Priest or Deacon celebrant, wearing an alb or surplice and stole, and even a cope, in a festive color, goes with the ministers to the door of the church, or to that part of the church where the parents and godparents are gathered with the child.

75. The celebrant greets those present, especially the parents and godparents, recalling in a few words the joy with which the parents received their child as a gift from God, who is the source of all life and who now wishes to bestow his own life on him (her). He may use these or similar words:

Dear parents and godparents:
Your family has experienced great joy at the birth of your child,
and the Church shares your happiness.
Today this joy has brought you to the Church
to give thanks to God for the gift of your child
and to celebrate a new birth in the waters of Baptism.
This community rejoices with you,
for today the number of those baptized in Christ will be increased,
and we offer you our support in raising your child
in the practice of the faith.
Therefore, brothers and sisters,
let us now prepare ourselves to participate in this celebration,
listening to God's Word, praying for this child and his (her) family,
and renewing our commitment to the Lord and to his people.

76. The celebrant first asks the parents of the child:

What name do you give (or: have you given) your child?

Parents:

N.

Celebrant:

What do you ask of God's Church for N.?

Parents:

Baptism.

The celebrant may use other words in this dialogue.

The first reply may be given by another person if, according to local custom, this person has the right to give the name.

In the second reply, the parents may use other words: e.g., Faith or The grace of Christ or Entry into the Church or Eternal life.

77. Then the celebrant addresses the parents in these or similar words:

**In asking for Baptism for your child,
you are undertaking the responsibility
of raising him (her) in the faith,
so that, keeping God's commandments,
he (she) may love the Lord and his (her) neighbor
    as Christ has taught us.
Do you understand this responsibility?**

Parents:

We do.

78. Then turning to the godparents, the celebrant asks in these or similar words:

Are you ready to help the parents of this child in their duty?

Godparents:

We are (I am).

79.   Then the celebrant continues, saying:

N., the Church of God receives you with great joy.
In her name I sign you with the Sign of the Cross
of Christ our Savior;
then, after me, your parents (and godparents) will do the same.

And, without saying anything, he signs the child on the forehead. Afterwards he invites the parents, and if it seems appropriate, the godparents, to do the same.

80.   The celebrant invites the parents, godparents, and others present to take part in the celebration of the Word of God. If circumstances permit, a procession to the appointed place takes place with singing (e.g., Psalm 85 [84]:7–9ab).

Psalm 85 (84):7–9ab

Will you not restore again our life,
    that your people may rejoice in you?
Show us, O Lord, your mercy,
    and grant us your salvation.
I will hear what the Lord God speaks;
    he speaks of peace for his people and his faithful.

Sacred Celebration of the Word of God

Biblical Readings and Homily

81.   If it seems appropriate, one, or even two, of the following passages is read, while all are seated.

Mt 28:18–20: *Go, therefore, and make disciples of all nations, baptizing them in the name of the Father, and of the Son, and of the Holy Spirit* (no. 205).

Mk 1:9–11: *Jesus was baptized in the Jordan by John* (no. 206).

Mk 10:13–16: *Let the children come to me; do not prevent them* (no. 207).

Jn 3:1–6: *No one can see the Kingdom of God without being born from above* (no. 209).

The passages that are to be found at nos. 186–194 and 204–215, or others suited to the wishes or needs of the parents, may also be chosen.

Between the Readings, the Responsorial Psalms or the Verses provided in nos. 195–203 may be sung.

82.   After the Reading, the celebrant preaches a brief homily in which light is shed on what has been read, and those present are led to a deeper understanding of the mystery of Baptism and to a more eager fulfill-ment of the responsibility that arises from it, especially for parents and godparents.

83.   After the Homily, or after the Litany, or even during the Litany, it is recommended that there be a period of silence in which all, invited by the celebrant, pray in their hearts. There follows, if the situation warrants, a suitable liturgical song, chosen, for example, from among those provided in nos. 225–245.

Prayer of the Faithful

84.   Then the Prayer of the Faithful takes place.

Celebrant:

Dear brothers and sisters,
let us invoke the mercy of our Lord Jesus Christ
for this child about to receive the grace of Baptism,
and for his (her) parents, godparents, and all the baptized.

Lector:

Give this child new birth in Baptism
through the radiant divine mystery of your Death and Resurrection,
and join him (her) to your holy Church:

All:

Lord, we ask you, hear our prayer.

Lector:

Make him (her) a faithful disciple and witness to your Gospel
through Baptism and Confirmation:

All:

Lord, we ask you, hear our prayer.

Lector:

**Lead him (her) through holiness of life
to the joys of the heavenly Kingdom:**

All:

Lord, we ask you, hear our prayer.

Lector:

**Make his (her) parents and godparents
a shining example of the faith to this child:**

All:

Lord, we ask you, hear our prayer.

Lector:

Keep his (her) family always in your love:

All:

Lord, we ask you, hear our prayer.

Lector:

Renew the grace of Baptism in each of us:

All:

Lord, we ask you, hear our prayer.

Other optional formulas, nos. 217–220.

85.   Afterwards, the celebrant invites those present to invoke the aid of the Saints:

Holy Mary, Mother of God,	pray for us.
Saint John the Baptist,	pray for us.
Saint Joseph,	pray for us.
Saint Peter and Saint Paul,	pray for us.

It is good to add the names of other Saints, especially the Patron Saint of the child or of the church or of the place. Then the Litany concludes:

All holy men and women, Saints of God,	pray for us.

Optional extended form of the Litany, no. 220A.

86. After the invocations, the celebrant says:

Almighty ever-living God,
who sent your Son into the world
to drive out from us the power of Satan, the spirit of evil,
and bring the human race, rescued from darkness,
into the marvelous Kingdom of your light:
we humbly beseech you
to free this child from Original Sin,
to make him (her) the temple of your glory,
and to grant that your Holy Spirit may dwell in him (her).
Through Christ our Lord.

All:

Amen.

Another formula for the Prayer of Exorcism, no. 221.

87. The celebrant continues:

May the strength of Christ the Savior protect you.
As a sign of this we anoint you with the oil of salvation
in the same Christ our Lord,
who lives and reigns for ever and ever.

All:

Amen.

The celebrant anoints the child on the breast with the Oil of Catechumens.

88. In the United States, if, for serious reasons, the celebrant judges it
pastorally necessary or desirable, the Anointing before Baptism may
be omitted. In that case, the celebrant says:

May the strength of Christ the Savior protect you;
who lives and reigns for ever and ever.

All:

Amen.

And immediately, without saying anything, he lays his hand on the child.

89.   Then they proceed to the baptistery, or, if circumstances suggest, to the sanctuary, if the Baptism is celebrated there.

CELEBRATION OF BAPTISM

90.   When they have come to the font, the celebrant briefly reminds those present of the wonderful plan of God, who willed to sanctify the human soul and body through water. He may do this in these or similar words:

Let us pray, dear brothers and sisters,
that the Lord God Almighty may bestow new life on this child
by water and the Holy Spirit.

Or:

Dear brothers and sisters,
you know that God graciously bestows
his abundant life through the sacrament of water
on those who believe.
Let us then raise our minds to him,
and with one heart pray
that he may be pleased to pour out his grace from this font
upon this chosen one.

BLESSING OF WATER AND INVOCATION OF GOD OVER THE WATER

91.   Then, turning to the font, the celebrant says the following Blessing (outside Easter Time):

O God, who by invisible power
accomplish a wondrous effect
through sacramental signs
and who in many ways have prepared water, your creation,
to show forth the grace of Baptism;

O God, whose Spirit
in the first moments of the world's creation
hovered over the waters,
so that the very substance of water
would even then take to itself the power to sanctify;

O God, who by the outpouring of the flood
foreshadowed regeneration,
so that from the mystery of one and the same element of water
would come an end to vice and a beginning of virtue;

O God, who caused the children of Abraham
to pass dry-shod through the Red Sea,
so that the chosen people,
set free from slavery to Pharaoh,
would prefigure the people of the baptized;

O God, whose Son,
baptized by John in the waters of the Jordan,
was anointed with the Holy Spirit,
and, as he hung upon the Cross,
gave forth water from his side along with blood,
and after his Resurrection, commanded his disciples:
"Go forth, teach all nations, baptizing them
in the name of the Father and of the Son and of the Holy Spirit,"
look now, we pray, upon the face of your Church
and graciously unseal for her the fountain of Baptism.

May this water receive by the Holy Spirit
the grace of your Only Begotten Son,
so that human nature, created in your image
and washed clean through the Sacrament of Baptism
from all the squalor of the life of old,
may be found worthy to rise to the life of newborn children
through water and the Holy Spirit.

The celebrant touches the water with his right hand and continues:

May the power of the Holy Spirit,
O Lord, we pray,
come down through your Son
into the fullness of this font,
so that all who have been buried with Christ
by Baptism into death
may rise again to life with him.
Who lives and reigns for ever and ever.

All:

Amen.

Other optional formulas, nos. 223–224.

92.   During Easter Time, however, if the baptismal water has been consecrated at the Easter Vigil, so that the Baptism may not lack the element of thanksgiving and petition, the blessing and invocation of God over the water takes place in accordance with the formulas found in nos. 223–224, using the textual variation given at the end of these same formulas.

Renunciation of Sin and Profession of Faith

93.   The celebrant instructs the parents and godparents in these words:

Dear parents and godparents:
through the Sacrament of Baptism
the child you have presented
is about to receive from the love of God
new life by water and the Holy Spirit.

For your part, you must strive to bring him (her) up in the faith,
so that this divine life may be preserved from the contagion of sin,
and may grow in him (her) day by day.

If your faith makes you ready to accept this responsibility,
then, mindful of your own Baptism,
renounce sin and profess faith in Christ Jesus,
the faith of the Church,
in which children are baptized.

94.   Then the celebrant questions the parents and godparents:

Do you renounce Satan?

Parents and godparents:

I do.

Celebrant:

And all his works?

Parents and godparents:

I do.

Celebrant:

And all his empty show?

Parents and godparents:

I do.

Or:

Celebrant:

**Do you renounce sin,
so as to live in the freedom of the children of God?**

Parents and godparents:

I do.

Celebrant:

**Do you renounce the lure of evil,
so that sin may have no mastery over you?**

Parents and godparents:

I do.

Celebrant:

**Do you renounce Satan,
the author and prince of sin?**

Parents and godparents:

I do.

In the United States, if the occasion requires, this second formula may be adapted with more precision by the Diocesan Bishop, especially when it is necessary that the parents and godparents should renounce superstitions, divinations, and magical arts practiced with reference to the child.

95. Next, the celebrant elicits the threefold profession of faith by the parents and godparents, saying:

Do you believe in God,
the Father almighty,
Creator of heaven and earth?

Parents and godparents:

I do.

Celebrant:

Do you believe in Jesus Christ, his only Son, our Lord,
who was born of the Virgin Mary,
suffered death and was buried,
rose again from the dead
and is seated at the right hand of the Father?

Parents and godparents:

I do.

Celebrant:

Do you believe in the Holy Spirit,
the holy catholic Church,
the communion of saints,
the forgiveness of sins,
the resurrection of the body,
and life everlasting?

Parents and godparents:

I do.

96. The celebrant, together with the community, gives assent to this profession of faith, saying:

This is our faith. This is the faith of the Church.
We are proud to profess it in Christ Jesus our Lord.

All:

Amen.

Another formula may be substituted, if circumstances suggest. Or a suitable liturgical song, by which the community expresses its faith with one voice, may be sung.

97.   The celebrant invites the family to approach the font. In addition, using the name of the child, he asks the parents and godparents:

Is it your will, therefore, that N. should receive Baptism in the faith of the Church, which we have all professed with you?

Parents and godparents:

It is.

And immediately the celebrant baptizes the child, saying:

N., I BAPTIZE YOU IN THE NAME OF THE FATHER,

He immerses the child or pours water over him (her) a first time.

AND OF THE SON,

He immerses the child or pours water over him (her) a second time.

AND OF THE HOLY SPIRIT.

He immerses the child or pours water over him (her) a third time.

After the Baptism of the child, it is appropriate for the people to sing a short acclamation, such as:

Blessed be God, who chose you in Christ.

Other optional acclamations, nos. 225–245.

If the Baptism is celebrated by the pouring of water, it is preferable for the child to be held by the mother (or by the father); however, where it is felt that the existing custom should be retained, the child may be held by the godmother (or by the godfather). If the Baptism is by immersion, the child is lifted from the sacred font by the same person.

Explanatory Rites

Anointing after Baptism

98.   Then the celebrant says:

Almighty God, the Father of our Lord Jesus Christ,
has freed you from sin,
given you new birth by water and the Holy Spirit,
and joined you to his people.
He now anoints you with the Chrism of salvation,
so that you may remain as a member of Christ,
 Priest, Prophet and King,
unto eternal life.

All:

Amen.

Then, without saying anything, the celebrant anoints the child with sacred Chrism on the crown of his (her) head.

Clothing with a White Garment

99.   The celebrant says:

N., you have become a new creation
and have clothed yourself in Christ.
May this white garment be a sign to you of your Christian dignity.
With your family and friends to help you by word and example,
bring it unstained into eternal life.

All:

Amen.

And a white garment is placed on the child; another color is not permitted, unless it is demanded by local custom. It is desirable that the family itself provide this garment.

100. The celebrant then takes the paschal candle and says:

Receive the light of Christ.

One member of the family (e.g., the father or godfather) lights a candle for the child from the paschal candle.

Then the celebrant says:

Parents and godparents,
this light is entrusted to you to be kept burning brightly,
so that your child, enlightened by Christ,
may walk always as a child of the light
and, persevering in the faith,
may run to meet the Lord when he comes
with all the Saints in the heavenly court.

"Ephphatha"

101. In the United States, the "Ephphatha" Rite takes place at the discretion of the celebrant. The celebrant touches the ears and mouth of the child with his thumb, saying:

May the Lord Jesus,
who made the deaf to hear and the mute to speak,
grant that you may soon receive his word with your ears
and profess the faith with your lips,
to the glory and praise of God the Father.

All:

Amen.

Conclusion of the Rite

102. Afterwards, unless the Baptism took place in the sanctuary, there is a procession to the altar, in which the lighted candle of the newly baptized child is carried.

Meanwhile, it is desirable that a baptismal canticle be sung, e.g.:

Baptized in Christ,
you are clothed with Christ,
alleluia, alleluia.

Other optional canticles, nos. 225–245.

Lord's Prayer

103. The celebrant, standing before the altar, addresses the parents and godparents and all present in these or similar words:

Dear brothers and sisters:
this child, reborn through Baptism,
is now called a child of God, for so indeed he (she) is.

Through Confirmation he (she) will receive the fullness
of the Holy Spirit
and, approaching the altar of the Lord,
he (she) will share at the table of his Sacrifice,
and will call upon God as Father in the midst of the Church.
Now in his (her) name,
and in the spirit of adoption as sons and daughters
which we have all received,
let us pray together as the Lord taught us.

104. And all say together with the celebrant:

Our Father, who art in heaven,
hallowed be thy name;
thy kingdom come,
thy will be done
on earth as it is in heaven.
Give us this day our daily bread,
and forgive us our trespasses,
as we forgive those who trespass against us;
and lead us not into temptation,
but deliver us from evil.

BLESSING AND DISMISSAL

105. Then the celebrant blesses the mother, holding her child in her arms, the father, and all those present, saying:

The Lord God Almighty,
through his Son, born of the Virgin Mary,
brings joy to Christian mothers
as the hope of eternal life shines forth upon their children.
May he graciously bless the mother of this child,
so that, as she now gives thanks for the gift of her child,
she may always remain united with him (her) in thanksgiving,
in Christ Jesus our Lord.

All:

Amen.

Celebrant:

May the Lord God Almighty,
the giver of life both in heaven and on earth,
bless the father of this child,
so that, together with his wife,
they may, by word and example,
prove to be the first witnesses of the faith to their child,
in Christ Jesus our Lord.

All:

Amen.

Celebrant:

**May the Lord God Almighty,
who by water and the Holy Spirit
has given us new birth into eternal life,
abundantly bless his faithful here present,
that always and everywhere they may be active members
 of his people;
and may he bestow his peace on all who are here,
in Christ Jesus our Lord.**

All:

Amen.

Celebrant:

**May almighty God bless you,
the Father, and the Son, ✛ and the Holy Spirit.**

All:

Amen.

Celebrant:

Go in peace.

All:

Thanks be to God.

Other optional formulas of blessing, nos. 247–249.

106. After the blessing, if circumstances suggest, a suitable canticle that expresses paschal joy and thanksgiving or the Canticle of the Blessed Virgin Mary, the **Magnificat**, may be sung by all.

Where it is the custom to bring the baptized infant to the altar of the Blessed Virgin Mary, this custom should appropriately be retained.

Chapter III

ORDER OF BAPTISM FOR A LARGE NUMBER OF CHILDREN

Rite of Receiving the Children

107. The faithful sing a suitable Psalm or hymn, if circumstances allow. Meanwhile, the Priest or Deacon celebrant, wearing an alb or surplice and stole, and even a cope, in a festive color, goes with the ministers to the door of the church, or to that part of the church where the parents and godparents are gathered with those to be baptized.

108. The celebrant greets those present, especially the parents and godparents, recalling in a few words the joy with which the parents received their children as a gift from God, who is the source of all life and who now wishes to bestow his own life on them. He may use these or similar words:

Dear parents and godparents:
Your families have experienced great joy at the birth
of your children,
and the Church shares your happiness.
Today this joy has brought you to the Church
to give thanks to God for the gift of your children
and to celebrate a new birth in the waters of Baptism.
This community rejoices with you,
for today the number of those baptized in Christ will be increased,
and we offer you our support in raising your children
in the practice of the faith.
Therefore, brothers and sisters,
let us now prepare ourselves to participate in this celebration,
listening to God's Word, praying for these children
and their families,
and renewing our commitment to the Lord and to his people.

Then he asks the parents and godparents all together:

What name do you give (or: have you given) your children?

Each family answers in turn, giving the name of the child.

Celebrant:

What do you ask of God's Church for them?

All the families together:

Baptism.

If, however, there are a very great number to be baptized, the first question is omitted and the celebrant immediately says:

Parents and godparents, who are present here with these children, what do you ask of God's Church for them?

All the families together:

Baptism.

---

109. Then the celebrant first addresses the parents:

Parents, in asking for Baptism for your children,
you are undertaking the responsibility
of raising them in the faith,
so that, keeping God's commandments,
they may love the Lord and their neighbor as Christ has taught us.
Do you understand this responsibility?

All the parents together:

We do.

110. Then turning to the godparents, the celebrant asks:

And you, the godparents,
are you ready to help the parents of these children in their duty?

All the godparents together:

We are.

111. Then the celebrant continues, saying:

Dear children,
the Church of God receives you with great joy.
In her name I sign you with the Sign of the Cross.

He makes the Sign of the Cross over all the children together, and says:

Parents (or: **Godparents**),
sign your children on the forehead
with the Sign of the Cross of Christ our Savior.

Then the parents (or godparents) sign the children on the forehead.

Sacred Celebration of the Word of God

Biblical Readings and Homily

112. The celebrant invites the parents and godparents and the others present to take part in the celebration of the Word of God. He may read verses 18–20 of chapter 28 of the Gospel according to Matthew, about the mission of the Apostles to preach the Gospel and to baptize (no. 205). Other passages, listed in nos. 44 or 186–194 and 204–215, may also be chosen.

113. After the Reading, the celebrant preaches a brief homily in which light is shed on what has been read, and those present are led to a deeper understanding of the mystery of Baptism and to a more eager fulfillment of the responsibility that arises from it, especially for parents and godparents.

PRAYER OF THE FAITHFUL

114. Then the Prayer of the Faithful takes place.

Celebrant:

Dear brothers and sisters,
let us invoke the mercy of our Lord Jesus Christ
for these children about to receive the grace of Baptism,
and for their parents, godparents, and all the baptized.

Lector:

Give these children new birth in Baptism
through the radiant divine mystery of your Death and Resurrection,
and join them to your holy Church:

All:

Lord, we ask you, hear our prayer.

Lector:

Make them faithful disciples and witnesses to your Gospel
through Baptism and Confirmation:

All:

Lord, we ask you, hear our prayer.

Lector:

Lead them through holiness of life
to the joys of the heavenly Kingdom:

All:

Lord, we ask you, hear our prayer.

Lector:

Make their parents and godparents
a shining example of the faith to these children:

All:

Lord, we ask you, hear our prayer.

Lector:

Keep their families always in your love:

All:

Lord, we ask you, hear our prayer.

Lector:

Renew the grace of Baptism in each of us:

All:

Lord, we ask you, hear our prayer.

Other optional formulas, nos. 217–220.

The Invocation of the Saints (Litany) may be omitted (cf. no. 48).

PRAYER OF EXORCISM

115. The Prayer of the Faithful concludes with the Prayer of Exorcism:

Almighty ever-living God,
who sent your Son into the world
to drive out from us the power of Satan, the spirit of evil,
and bring the human race, rescued from darkness,
into the marvelous Kingdom of your light:
we humbly beseech you
to free these children from Original Sin,
to make them the temple of your glory,
and to grant that your Holy Spirit may dwell in them.
Through Christ our Lord.

All:

Amen.

Another formula for the Prayer of Exorcism, no. 221.

And the celebrant, omitting the Anointing with the Oil of Catechumens because of the number to be baptized, lays hands over all the children at once, saying:

May the strength of Christ the Savior protect you;
who lives and reigns for ever and ever.

All:

Amen.

116. Then they proceed to the place in which the Baptism is celebrated.

CELEBRATION OF BAPTISM

BLESSING OF WATER AND INVOCATION OF GOD OVER THE WATER

117. Standing at the font, the celebrant briefly reminds those present of the wonderful plan of God, who willed to sanctify the human soul and body through water. He may do this in these or similar words:

Through the sacrament of water
God bestows his life on those who believe.
Let us therefore be strong in faith,
praying to him with one heart,
that these children may be born again
of water and the Holy Spirit.

118. Then, turning to the font, the celebrant says the following blessing:

Most merciful Father,
from the font of Baptism,
you have made the new life of your children
well up within us.

All:

Blessed be God.

(Or another suitable acclamation of the people.)

Celebrant:

You have been pleased to unite
by water and the Holy Spirit
all the baptized into one people in your Son Jesus Christ.

All:

Blessed be God.

Celebrant:

You free us by the Spirit of your love,
whom you pour into our hearts,
so that we may delight in your peace.

All:

Blessed be God.

Celebrant:

You choose the baptized,
that they may joyfully proclaim to all the nations
the Gospel of your Christ.

All:

Blessed be God.

Celebrant:

* Be pleased now to bless ✛ this water,
by which your servants are to be baptized,
for you have called them to this cleansing water of rebirth
in the faith of the Church,
that they may have eternal life.
Through Christ our Lord.

All:

Amen.

119. * But when, during Easter Time, there is baptismal water already blessed at hand, the celebrant omits the last part of the preceding blessing Be pleased now to bless this water and concludes as follows:

By the mystery of this blessed water,
graciously lead to spiritual rebirth your servants,
whom you have called to this cleansing in the faith of the Church,
that they may have eternal life.
Through Christ our Lord.

All:

Amen.

Other optional formulas, nos. 222–223.

Renunciation of Sin and Profession of Faith

120. The celebrant instructs the parents and godparents in these words:

Dear parents and godparents:
through the Sacrament of Baptism
the children you have presented
are about to receive from the love of God
new life by water and the Holy Spirit.

For your part, you must strive to bring them up in the faith,
so that this divine life may be preserved from the contagion of sin,
and may grow in them day by day.

If your faith makes you ready to accept this responsibility,
then, mindful of your own Baptism,
renounce sin and profess faith in Christ Jesus,
the faith of the Church,
in which children are baptized.

121.   Then the celebrant questions them:

Do you renounce Satan?

Parents and godparents:

I do.

Celebrant:

And all his works?

Parents and godparents:

I do.

Celebrant:

And all his empty show?

Parents and godparents:

I do.

Or:

Celebrant:

**Do you renounce sin,
so as to live in the freedom of the children of God?**

Parents and godparents:

I do.

Celebrant:

**Do you renounce the lure of evil,
so that sin may have no mastery over you?**

Parents and godparents:

I do.

**Do you renounce Satan,
the author and prince of sin?**

Parents and godparents:

I do.

In the United States, if the occasion requires, this second formula may
be adapted with more precision by the Diocesan Bishop, especially when
it is necessary that the parents and godparents should renounce superstitions, divinations, and magical arts practiced with reference to the
children.

122. Next, the celebrant elicits the threefold profession of faith by the
parents and godparents, saying:

**Do you believe in God,
the Father almighty,
Creator of heaven and earth?**

Parents and godparents:

I do.

Celebrant:

**Do you believe in Jesus Christ, his only Son, our Lord,
who was born of the Virgin Mary,
suffered death and was buried,
rose again from the dead
and is seated at the right hand of the Father?**

Parents and godparents:

I do.

Celebrant:

**Do you believe in the Holy Spirit,
the holy catholic Church,
the communion of saints,
the forgiveness of sins,
the resurrection of the body,
and life everlasting?**

Parents and godparents:

I do.

123. The celebrant, together with the community, gives assent to this profession of faith, saying:

This is our faith. This is the faith of the Church.
We are proud to profess it in Christ Jesus our Lord.

All:

Amen.

Another formula may be substituted, if circumstances suggest. Or a suitable liturgical song, by which the community expresses its faith with one voice, may be sung.

Baptism

124. When because of the number of children to be baptized there are several ministers, each of them, using the name of the child to be baptized, questions the parents and godparents, saying:

Is it your will, therefore, that N. should receive Baptism in the faith of the Church, which we have all professed with you?

Parents and godparents:

It is.

And immediately the minister baptizes the child, saying:

N., I baptize you in the name of the Father,

He immerses the child or pours water over him (her) a first time.

and of the Son,

He immerses the child or pours water over him (her) a second time.

and of the Holy Spirit.

He immerses the child or pours water over him (her) a third time.

He asks the same question and does the same for each child to be baptized.

If the Baptism is celebrated by the pouring of water, it is preferable for the child to be held by the mother (or by the father); however, where it is felt that the existing custom should be retained, the child may be held by the godmother (or by the godfather). If the Baptism is by immersion, the child is lifted from the sacred font by the same person.

While the children are being baptized, the community may sing acclamations or liturgical songs, such as:

Blessed be God, who chose you in Christ.

Other optional acclamations, nos. 225–245. There may also be scriptural readings, or a sacred silence may be observed.

Explanatory Rites

Anointing after Baptism

125. In the United States, the Anointing after Baptism may not be omitted, even if very many children are baptized. The principal celebrant says the formula for Anointing once on behalf of all:

Almighty God, the Father of our Lord Jesus Christ,
has freed you from sin,
given you new birth by water and the Holy Spirit,
and joined you to his people.
He now anoints you with the Chrism of salvation,
so that you may remain members of Christ,
 Priest, Prophet and King,
unto eternal life.

All:

Amen.

Then, without saying anything, the ministers anoint each baptized child with sacred Chrism on the crown of his (her) head.

Clothing with a White Garment

126. The principal celebrant says:

**Dear children, you have become a new creation
and have clothed yourselves in Christ.
May this white garment be a sign to you of your Christian dignity.
With your family and friends to help you by word and example,
bring it unstained into eternal life.**

All:

Amen.

And a white garment is placed on each child; another color is not permitted, unless it is demanded by local custom. It is desirable that the families themselves provide this garment.

Handing On of a Lighted Candle

127. The principal celebrant then takes the paschal candle and says:

**Receive the light of Christ.
Parents and godparents,
this light is entrusted to you to be kept burning brightly,
so that your children, enlightened by Christ,
may walk always as children of the light
and, persevering in the faith,
may run to meet the Lord when he comes
with all the Saints in the heavenly court.**

Candles are given to each family, and lit from the paschal candle. The light is taken by the head of one family and passed on to all. Meanwhile, the community may sing a baptismal canticle, e.g.:

**Baptized in Christ,
you are clothed with Christ,
alleluia, alleluia.**

Other optional canticles, nos. 225–245.

Meanwhile, unless the Baptism took place in the sanctuary, there is a procession to the altar, in which the lighted candles of the newly baptized are carried.

CONCLUSION OF THE RITE

LORD'S PRAYER

128. The celebrant, standing before the altar, addresses the parents and godparents and all present in these or similar words:

Dear brothers and sisters:
these children, reborn through Baptism,
are now called children of God, for so indeed they are.

Through Confirmation they will receive the fullness
    of the Holy Spirit
and, approaching the altar of the Lord,
they will share at the table of his Sacrifice,
and will call upon God as Father in the midst of the Church.
Now in their name,
and in the spirit of adoption as sons and daughters
which we have all received,
let us pray together as the Lord taught us.

129. And all say together:

Our Father, who art in heaven,
hallowed be thy name;
thy kingdom come,
thy will be done
on earth as it is in heaven.
Give us this day our daily bread,
and forgive us our trespasses,
as we forgive those who trespass against us;
and lead us not into temptation,
but deliver us from evil.

130. Then the celebrant blesses and dismisses those present, saying:

Brothers and sisters,
we commend you to the mercies and grace
of God the almighty Father,
of his Only Begotten Son,
and of the Holy Spirit.
May he guard your life,
so that, walking in the light of faith,
you may come to the good things that are promised
and we together with you.

All:

Amen.

Celebrant:

May almighty God bless you,
the Father, and the Son, ✝ and the Holy Spirit.

All:

Amen.

Celebrant:

Go in peace.

All:

Thanks be to God.

Other optional formulas of blessing, nos. 70, 247–248.

131. After the blessing, if circumstances suggest, a suitable canticle that expresses paschal joy and thanksgiving or the Canticle of the Blessed Virgin Mary, the **Magnificat**, may be sung by all.

Chapter IV

ORDER OF BAPTISM OF CHILDREN TO BE USED BY CATECHISTS IN THE ABSENCE OF A PRIEST OR DEACON

Rite of Receiving the Children

132. The faithful sing a suitable Psalm or hymn, if circumstances allow. Meanwhile, the catechist goes with the ministers to the door of the church, or to that part of the church where the parents and godparents are gathered with those to be baptized.

If there are very many children to be baptized, the catechist may be assisted by others in the act of Baptism, as noted below.

133. The catechist greets those present, especially the parents and god-parents, recalling in a few words the joy with which the parents received their children as a gift from God, who is the source of all life and who now wishes to bestow his own life on them. The catechist may use these or similar words:

Dear parents and godparents:
Your families have experienced great joy at the birth
of your children,
and the Church shares your happiness.
Today this joy has brought you to the Church
to give thanks to God for the gift of your children
and to celebrate a new birth in the waters of Baptism.
This community rejoices with you,
for today the number of those baptized in Christ will be increased,
and we offer you our support in raising your children
in the practice of the faith.
Therefore, brothers and sisters,
let us now prepare ourselves to participate in this celebration,
listening to God's Word, praying for these children
and their families,
and renewing our commitment to the Lord and to his people.

Then the catechist asks the parents and godparents all together in these or similar words:

What name do you give (or: have you given) your children?

Each family answers in turn, giving the name of the child.

Catechist:

What do you ask of God's Church for them?

All the families together:

Baptism.

If, however, there are a very great number to be baptized, the first question is omitted and the catechist immediately says:

Parents and godparents, who are present here with these children, what do you ask of God's Church for them?

All the families together:

Baptism.

---

134. Then the catechist first addresses the parents:

Parents, in asking for Baptism for your children,
you are undertaking the responsibility
of raising them in the faith,
so that, keeping God's commandments,
they may love the Lord and their neighbor as Christ has taught us.
Do you understand this responsibility?

All the parents together:

We do.

135. Then turning to the godparents, the catechist asks:

And you, the godparents,
are you ready to help the parents of these children in their duty?

All the godparents together:

We are.

136. Then the catechist continues, saying:

Dear children,
the Church of God receives you with great joy.
In her name I sign you with the Sign of the Cross.

The catechist makes the Sign of the Cross over all the children together,
and says:

Parents (or: **Godparents**),
sign your children on the forehead
with the Sign of the Cross of Christ our Savior.

Then the parents (or godparents) sign the children on the forehead.

SACRED CELEBRATION OF THE WORD OF GOD

READING AND HOMILY OR INSTRUCTION

137. The catechist invites the parents and godparents and the others
present to take part in the celebration of the Word of God. Verses 18–
20 of chapter 28 of the Gospel according to Matthew, about the mission of the Apostles to preach the Gospel and to baptize, may be read
(no. 205), or the passages listed at nos. 186–194 and 204–215. Psalms
and liturgical songs, if required, may be found at nos. 195–203. After
the Reading a brief homily may be given by the catechist, in a manner
determined by the Bishop.

138. In place of the biblical Reading and Homily mentioned above,
the catechist, in case of necessity, may read this instruction:

When Christ sent out his Apostles with these words:
"Go forth, teach all the nations, baptizing them
in the name of the Father and of the Son and of the Holy Spirit,"
he entrusted Baptism to his Church,
by which he will come to meet these children.

In such a great Sacrament, children are set free from sin,
become members of the Church and sons and daughters of God,
and so, as you know, will be graced with countless gifts.
Since all these things are wholly beyond human reach,
they must be humbly sought in faith by our assembly.

And God our Father,
hearing the voice of Christ in our common prayer
and recognizing the faith of the Church,
will now, in the power of his Holy Spirit,
bestow on these beloved children
what he has promised at the coming of his Son.

PRAYER OF THE FAITHFUL

139. Then the Prayer of the Faithful takes place.

Catechist:

Dear brothers and sisters,
let us invoke the mercy of our Lord Jesus Christ
for these children about to receive the grace of Baptism,
and for their parents, godparents, and all the baptized.

Lector:

Give these children new birth in Baptism
through the radiant divine mystery of your Death and Resurrection,
and join them to your holy Church:

All:

Lord, we ask you, hear our prayer.

Lector:

Make them faithful disciples and witnesses to your Gospel
through Baptism and Confirmation:

All:

Lord, we ask you, hear our prayer.

Lector:

Lead them through holiness of life
to the joys of the heavenly Kingdom:

All:

Lord, we ask you, hear our prayer.

Lector:

**Make their parents and godparents
a shining example of the faith to these children:**

All:

Lord, we ask you, hear our prayer.

Lector:

Keep their families always in your love:

All:

Lord, we ask you, hear our prayer.

Lector:

Renew the grace of Baptism in each of us:

All:

Lord, we ask you, hear our prayer.

Other optional formulas, nos. 217–220.

140. Afterwards, the catechist invites those present to invoke the Saints:

Holy Mary, Mother of God,	pray for us.
Saint John the Baptist,	pray for us.
Saint Joseph,	pray for us.
Saint Peter and Saint Paul,	pray for us.

It is good to add the names of other Saints, especially those who are Patron Saints of the children or of the church or of the place. Then the Litany concludes:

All holy men and women, Saints of God,	pray for us.

Optional extended form of the Litany, no. 220A.

The Prayer of Exorcism and the Anointing before Baptism with the Oil of Catechumens are omitted.

Celebration of Baptism

Blessing of Water and Invocation of God over the Water

141. The catechist with the parents and godparents, carrying the children to be baptized, go to the baptismal font.

Then the catechist invites those present to pray with these words:

Let us pray, dear brothers and sisters,
that the Lord God Almighty may bestow new life on these children
by water and the Holy Spirit.

142. If there is no blessed water at hand, the catechist, standing before the font, proclaims this invocation:

Most merciful Father,
from the font of Baptism,
you have made the new life of your children
well up within us.

All:

Blessed be God.

(Or another suitable acclamation of the people.)

Catechist:

You have been pleased to unite
by water and the Holy Spirit
all the baptized into one people in your Son Jesus Christ.

All:

Blessed be God.

Catechist:

You free us by the Spirit of your love,
whom you pour into our hearts,
so that we may delight in your peace.

All:

Blessed be God.

Catechist:

You choose the baptized,
that they may joyfully proclaim to all the nations
the Gospel of your Christ.

All:

Blessed be God.

Catechist:

Be pleased now to bless this water,
by which your servants are to be baptized,
for you have called them to this cleansing water of rebirth
in the faith of the Church,
that they may have eternal life.
Through Christ our Lord.

All:

Amen.

143. But if there is water already blessed at hand, the catechist says the
following invocation:

O God, fount of all life and love,
Father of our Lord Jesus Christ,
you are glorified in the joys and anxieties of parents.

In the birth of children,
you prefigure the newness of your wonders,
and in their rebirth to eternal life,
you reveal the surpassing fruitfulness of your Son.

Mercifully hear the prayers of these parents and of the Church,
and embrace these children with your love.

Let them not be bound by the rule of sin,
but because they come from you,
in mercy take them into the Kingdom of your Son.

You prepared water for the cleansing, life,
and refreshment of your creatures,
and were pleased to sanctify it through the Baptism of Christ,
so that all may be born from above.

By water, and the power and working of the Holy Spirit,
grant that these children,
baptized into the mystery of the Passion and Resurrection
    of your Christ,
may receive adoption as your sons and daughters,
take part in your Church,
and for all eternity rejoice in your company,
with the Son and the Holy Spirit,
for ever and ever.

All:

Amen.

Renunciation of Sin and Profession of Faith

144. The catechist instructs the parents and godparents in these words:

Dear parents and godparents:
through the Sacrament of Baptism
the children you have presented
are about to receive from the love of God
new life by water and the Holy Spirit.

For your part, you must strive to bring them up in the faith,
so that this divine life may be preserved from the contagion of sin,
and may grow in them day by day.

If your faith makes you ready to accept this responsibility,
then, mindful of your own Baptism,
renounce sin and profess faith in Christ Jesus,
the faith of the Church,
in which children are baptized.

145. Then the catechist questions them:

Do you renounce Satan?

Parents and godparents:

I do.

Catechist:

And all his works?

Parents and godparents:

I do.

Catechist:

And all his empty show?

Parents and godparents:

I do.

Or:

Catechist:

**Do you renounce sin,
so as to live in the freedom of the children of God?**

Parents and godparents:

I do.

Catechist:

**Do you renounce the lure of evil,
so that sin may have no mastery over you?**

Parents and godparents:

I do.

Catechist:

**Do you renounce Satan,
the author and prince of sin?**

Parents and godparents:

I do.

In the United States, if the occasion requires, this second formula may be adapted with more precision by the Diocesan Bishop, especially when it is necessary that the parents and godparents should renounce superstitions, divinations, and magical arts practiced with reference to the children.

146. Next, the catechist elicits the threefold profession of faith by the parents and godparents, saying:

**Do you believe in God,
the Father almighty,
Creator of heaven and earth?**

Parents and godparents:

I do.

Catechist:

**Do you believe in Jesus Christ, his only Son, our Lord,
who was born of the Virgin Mary,
suffered death and was buried,
rose again from the dead
and is seated at the right hand of the Father?**

Parents and godparents:

I do.

Catechist:

**Do you believe in the Holy Spirit,
the holy catholic Church,
the communion of saints,
the forgiveness of sins,
the resurrection of the body,
and life everlasting?**

Parents and godparents:

I do.

147. The catechist, together with the community, gives assent to this profession of faith, saying:

**This is our faith. This is the faith of the Church.
We are proud to profess it in Christ Jesus our Lord.**

All:

Amen.

Another formula may be substituted, if circumstances suggest. Or a suitable liturgical song, by which the community expresses its faith with one voice, may be sung.

148. The catechist invites the first family to approach the font. In addition, using the name of the individual child, the catechist asks the parents and godparents:

Is it your will, therefore, that N. should receive Baptism in the faith of the Church, which we have all professed with you?

Parents and godparents:

It is.

And immediately the minister baptizes the child, saying:

N., I baptize you in the name of the Father,

The catechist immerses the child or pours water over him (her) a first time.

And of the Son,

The catechist immerses the child or pours water over him (her) a second time.

And of the Holy Spirit.

The catechist immerses the child or pours water over him (her) a third time.

If the Baptism is celebrated by the pouring of water, it is preferable for the child to be held by the mother (or by the father); however, where it is felt that the existing custom should be retained, the child may be held by the godmother (or by the godfather). If the Baptism is by immersion, the child is lifted from the sacred font by the same person.

149. If there are many children to be baptized, and there are several catechists present, each of them may baptize some of the children, by using the same method and formula described above (no. 148).

150. While the children are being baptized, the community may sing acclamations or liturgical songs (cf. nos. 225–245). There may also be scriptural readings, or a sacred silence may be observed.

Explanatory Rites

Postbaptismal Prayer

151. The Anointing with sacred Chrism is omitted. The catechist, however, says on behalf of all the baptized:

**May almighty God, the Father of our Lord Jesus Christ,
who has freed you from sin,
given you new birth by water and the Holy Spirit,
and joined you to his people,
grant that as you have now been made Christians,
you may remain members of Christ, Priest, Prophet and King,
unto eternal life.**

All:

Amen.

Clothing with a White Garment

152. The catechist says:

**Dear children, you have become a new creation
and have clothed yourselves in Christ.
May this white garment be a sign to you of your Christian dignity.
With your family and friends to help you by word and example,
bring it unstained into eternal life.**

All:

Amen.

And a white garment is placed on each child; another color is not permitted, unless it is demanded by local custom. It is desirable that the families themselves provide this garment.

153. The catechist then takes the paschal candle and says:

Receive the light of Christ.
Parents and godparents,
this light is entrusted to you to be kept burning brightly,
so that your children, enlightened by Christ,
may walk always as children of the light
and, persevering in the faith,
may run to meet the Lord when he comes
with all the Saints in the heavenly court.

Candles are given to each family, and lit from the paschal candle. The light is taken by the head of one family and passed on to all. Meanwhile, the community may sing a baptismal canticle, e.g.:

Baptized in Christ,
you are clothed with Christ,
alleluia, alleluia.

Other optional canticles, nos. 225–245.

Meanwhile, unless the Baptism took place in the sanctuary, there is a procession to the altar, in which the lighted candles of the newly baptized are carried.

Conclusion of the Rite

Lord's Prayer

154. The catechist, standing before the altar, addresses the parents and godparents and all present in these or similar words:

Dear brothers and sisters:
these children, reborn through Baptism,
are now called children of God, for so indeed they are.

Through Confirmation they will receive the fullness
    of the Holy Spirit
and, approaching the altar of the Lord,
they will share at the table of his Sacrifice,
and will call upon God as Father in the midst of the Church.
Now in their name,
and in the spirit of adoption as sons and daughters
which we have all received,
let us pray together as the Lord taught us.

155. And all say together:

Our Father, who art in heaven,
hallowed be thy name;
thy kingdom come,
thy will be done
on earth as it is in heaven.
Give us this day our daily bread,
and forgive us our trespasses,
as we forgive those who trespass against us;
and lead us not into temptation,
but deliver us from evil.

156. Then the catechist invokes God's blessing and dismisses those present, saying:

Brothers and sisters,
we commend you to the mercies and grace
of God the almighty Father,
of his Only Begotten Son,
and of the Holy Spirit.
May he guard your life,
so that, walking in the light of faith,
you may come to the good things that are promised
and we together with you.

All:

Amen.

Catechist:

Go in peace.

All:

Thanks be to God.

After the blessing, if circumstances suggest, a suitable canticle that expresses paschal joy and thanksgiving or the Canticle of the Blessed Virgin Mary, the **Magnificat**, may be sung by all.

Where it is the custom to bring the baptized infants to the altar of the Blessed Virgin Mary, this custom should appropriately be retained.

Chapter V

ORDER OF BAPTISM OF CHILDREN IN DANGER OF DEATH, OR AT THE POINT OF DEATH, TO BE USED IN THE ABSENCE OF A PRIEST OR DEACON

157. When water, even if not blessed, has been prepared, and with parents, godparents and, if possible, some friends and neighbors gathered around the sick child, a minister or some suitable member of the faithful begins a short Prayer of the Faithful:

**Let us invoke the mercy of almighty God
for this child about to receive the grace of Baptism,
and for his (her) parents, godparents, and all the baptized.**

Unite this child to your Church through Baptism:

R.   Lord, we ask you, hear our prayer.

Grant him (her) adoption as your son (daughter) through Baptism:

R.   Lord, we ask you, hear our prayer.

**Grant him (her), who is to be buried with Christ in death
      through Baptism,
likewise to share in his Resurrection:**

R.   Lord, we ask you, hear our prayer.

Renew the grace of Baptism in all those gathered here:

R.   Lord, we ask you, hear our prayer.

**Keep all Christ's disciples, baptized into one body,
together always in faith and love:**

R.   Lord, we ask you, hear our prayer.

O God, fount of all life and love,
Father of our Lord Jesus Christ,
in relieving the anxiety of parents
and providing for children in peril,
you reveal your loving design in their rebirth to eternal life.

Listen with compassion to our prayer:
let this child not be held under the sway of sin,
but in mercy receive him (her) into the Kingdom of your Son.

And so, by water and by the power and working of the Holy Spirit,
grant that this child, to whom we give the name N.,
conformed to the mystery of the Death of your Christ
and configured to his Resurrection,
may receive adoption as your son (daughter)
and obtain the inheritance of Christ.

May he (she) enjoy in the Church
your communion
with your Only Begotten Son and the Holy Spirit,
for ever and ever.

R. Amen.

159. Then the profession of faith takes place. The minister invites those present with these words:

Mindful of our own Baptism,
let us profess faith in Christ Jesus,
the faith of the Church,
in which children are baptized.

Then the minister asks:

Do you believe in God,
the Father almighty,
Creator of heaven and earth?

R. I do.

Do you believe in Jesus Christ, his only Son, our Lord,
who was born of the Virgin Mary,
suffered death and was buried,
rose again from the dead
and is seated at the right hand of the Father?

R.   I do.

Do you believe in the Holy Spirit,
the holy catholic Church,
the communion of saints,
the forgiveness of sins,
the resurrection of the body,
and life everlasting?

R.   I do.

> The profession of faith may be made, if circumstances suggest, also by
> the recitation of the Apostles' Creed:

I believe in God,
the Father almighty,
Creator of heaven and earth,
and in Jesus Christ, his only Son, our Lord,
who was conceived by the Holy Spirit,
born of the Virgin Mary,
suffered under Pontius Pilate,
was crucified, died and was buried;
he descended into hell;
on the third day he rose again from the dead;
he ascended into heaven,
and is seated at the right hand of God the Father almighty;
from there he will come to judge the living and the dead.

I believe in the Holy Spirit,
the holy catholic Church,
the communion of saints,
the forgiveness of sins,
the resurrection of the body,
and life everlasting. Amen.

160. Then the minister baptizes the child, saying:

N., I BAPTIZE YOU IN THE NAME OF THE FATHER,

The minister pours water a first time.

AND OF THE SON,

The minister pours water a second time.

AND OF THE HOLY SPIRIT.

The minister pours water a third time.

161. The other rites are omitted and the Clothing with a White Garment may take place. The minister says:

N., you have become a new creation
and have clothed yourself in Christ.
May this white garment be a sign to you of your Christian dignity.
Bring it unstained into eternal life.

R.   Amen.

LORD'S PRAYER

162. The celebration concludes with the recitation of the Lord's Prayer:

Our Father, who art in heaven,
hallowed be thy name;
thy kingdom come,
thy will be done
on earth as it is in heaven.
Give us this day our daily bread,
and forgive us our trespasses,
as we forgive those who trespass against us;
and lead us not into temptation,
but deliver us from evil.

163. If there is no one among those present who is capable of leading prayer, any member of the faithful may baptize the child by reciting the Profession of Faith and afterwards by pouring water over the child to be baptized, with the appropriate words (cf. no. 160, above). However, even the recitation of the Profession of Faith, if circumstances suggest, may be omitted.

164. At the moment of death, omitting the other rites, it suffices that the minister pours water over the child, saying the appropriate words (cf. no. 160, above). It is desirable that the minister, if possible, has one or even a second witness present.

Chapter VI

ORDER OF BRINGING A BAPTIZED CHILD TO THE CHURCH

Rite of Receiving the Child

165. The faithful sing a suitable Psalm or hymn, if circumstances allow. Meanwhile, the Priest or Deacon celebrant, wearing an alb or surplice and stole, and even a cope, in a festive color, goes with the ministers to the door of the church, or to that part of the church where the parents and godparents are gathered with the child.

166. The celebrant greets those present, especially the parents and godparents, and praises them for having had the child baptized without delay, and gives thanks to God and congratulates the parents on the child's return to health.

167. The celebrant first asks the parents:

What name have you given your child?

Parents:

N.

Celebrant:

**Since he (she) has already been baptized,
what do you now ask of God's Church for N.?**

Parents:

That in the presence of the community,
it may be known that he (she) has been received into the Church.

The first reply may be given by another person, if according to local custom, this person has the right to give the name.

In the second reply, the parents may use other words: e.g., that he (she) is a Christian, or that he (she) has been baptized, etc.

168. Then the celebrant addresses the parents in these or similar words:

In bringing N. to the church,
you are undertaking the responsibility
of raising him (her) in the faith,
so that, keeping God's commandments,
he (she) may love the Lord and his (her) neighbor
as Christ has taught us.
Do you understand this responsibility?

Parents:

We do.

169. Then, turning to the godparents, the celebrant asks in these or similar words:

And you, the godparents,
are you ready to help the parents of this child in their duty?

Godparents:

We are (I am).

170. Then the celebrant continues, saying:

N., with great joy the Church of God
gives thanks with your parents,
welcomes you,
and testifies that you have already been received by the Church.

In her name I sign you with the Sign of the Cross of Christ,
who has bestowed life upon you in Baptism and joined you
to his Church.
And your parents (and godparents) will do the same.

And, without saying anything, he signs the child on the forehead. Afterwards he invites the parents, and, if it seems appropriate, the godparents, to do the same.

171. The celebrant invites the parents, godparents, and others present to take part in the celebration of the Word of God. If circumstances permit, a procession to the appointed place takes place with singing (e.g., Psalm 85 [84]:7–9ab).

Psalm 85 (84):7–9ab

Will you not restore again our life,
    that your people may rejoice in you?
Show us, O Lord, your mercy,
    and grant us your salvation.
I will hear what the Lord God speaks;
    he speaks of peace for his people and his faithful.

Sacred Celebration of the Word of God

Biblical Readings and Homily

172. If it seems appropriate, one, or even two, of the following passages is read, while all are seated.

Mt 28:18–20: *Go, therefore, and make disciples of all nations, baptizing them in the name of the Father, and of the Son, and of the Holy Spirit* (no. 205).

Mk 1:9–11: *Jesus was baptized in the Jordan by John* (no. 206).

Mk 10:13–16: *Let the children come to me; do not prevent them* (no. 207).

Jn 3:1–6: *No one can see the Kingdom of God without being born from above* (no. 209).

The passages that are to be found at nos. **186–194** and **204–215**, or others suited to the wishes or needs of the parents, may also be chosen (e.g., 1 Kings 17:17–24; 2 Kings 4:8–37).

Between the Readings, the Responsorial Psalms or the Verses provided in nos. **195–203** may be sung.

173. After the Reading, the celebrant preaches a brief homily in which light is shed on what has been read, and those present are led to a deeper understanding of the mystery of Baptism and to a more eager fulfillment of the responsibility that arises from it, especially for parents and godparents.

174. After the Homily, or after the Litany, or even during the Litany, it is recommended that there be a period of silence in which all, invited by the celebrant, pray in their hearts. There follows, if the situation warrants, a suitable liturgical song, chosen, for example, from among those found in nos. 225–245.

PRAYER OF THE FAITHFUL

175. Then the Prayer of the Faithful takes place.

Celebrant:

**To Christ, who is gracious and merciful,
let us pray for this child, for his (her) parents and godparents,
and for all the baptized.**

Lector:

**That this child may be mindful of his (her) Baptism
and restoration to health by God:**

All:

Lord, we ask you, hear our prayer.

Lector:

**That he (she) may always remain an active member
of your holy Church:**

All:

Lord, we ask you, hear our prayer.

Lector:

**That he (she) may come to hear your Gospel,
to abide by it, and to bear witness to it:**

All:

Lord, we ask you, hear our prayer.

Lector:

That he (she) may come joyfully to the table of your Sacrifice:

All:

Lord, we ask you, hear our prayer.

Lector:

That he (she) may love the Lord God and his (her) neighbor, as you have taught:

All:

Lord, we ask you, hear our prayer.

Lector:

That, instructed by the word and example of Christians, he (she) may grow in holiness and wisdom:

All:

Lord, we ask you, hear our prayer.

Lector:

That all your disciples may live always united in faith and love:

All:

Lord, we ask you, hear our prayer.

176. Afterwards, the celebrant invites those present to invoke the aid of the Saints:

Holy Mary, Mother of God,	pray for us.
Saint John the Baptist,	pray for us.
Saint Joseph,	pray for us.
Saint Peter and Saint Paul,	pray for us.

It is good to add the names of other Saints, especially the Patron Saint of the child or of the church or of the place. Then the Litany concludes:

All holy men and women, Saints of God,	pray for us.

Optional extended form of the Litany, no. 220A.

O God, fount of all life and love,
Father of our Lord Jesus Christ,
you display your glory in the loving concern of parents,
you show your provident care to children in peril,
and you reveal yourself as a savior in their Baptism.

The Church gives you thanks
that you have brought your servant N. out of the kingdom
    of darkness
into your wonderful light,
and have made him (her) a son (daughter) of adoption
and a temple of the Holy Spirit
by the Sacrament of Baptism.

And so the Church prays that you will always help him (her)
    in the perils of this life,
and continually fortify him (her) with the strength
    of Christ the Savior
in the struggle to gain your Kingdom.
Through Christ our Lord.

All:

Amen.

Explanatory Rites

Anointing after Baptism

178. Then the celebrant says:

Almighty God, the Father of our Lord Jesus Christ,
has freed you from sin,
given you new birth by water and the Holy Spirit,
and joined you to his people.
He now anoints you with the Chrism of salvation,
so that you may remain as a member of Christ,
    Priest, Prophet and King,
unto eternal life.

All:

Amen.

> Then, without saying anything, the celebrant anoints the child with
> sacred Chrism on the crown of his (her) head.

CLOTHING WITH A WHITE GARMENT

> 179. The celebrant says:

N., you have become a new creation
and have clothed yourself in Christ.
May this white garment be a sign to you of your Christian dignity.
With your family and friends to help you by word and example,
bring it unstained into eternal life.

> All:

Amen.

HANDING ON OF A LIGHTED CANDLE

> 180. The celebrant then takes the paschal candle and says:

Receive the light of Christ.

> One member of the family (e.g., the father or godfather) lights a candle
> for the child from the paschal candle.

> Then the celebrant says:

Parents and godparents,
this light is entrusted to you to be kept burning brightly,
so that your child, enlightened by Christ,
may walk always as a child of the light
and, persevering in the faith,
may run to meet the Lord when he comes
with all the Saints in the heavenly court.

> If circumstances suggest, the baptismal canticle Baptized in Christ
> (no. 67), or another of those that is found in nos. 225–245 may be sung.

Conclusion of the Rite

Lord's Prayer

181. The celebrant, standing before the altar, addresses the parents and godparents and all present in these or similar words:

Dear brothers and sisters:
this child, reborn through Baptism,
is now called a child of God, for so indeed he (she) is.

Through Confirmation he (she) will receive the fullness
    of the Holy Spirit
and, approaching the altar of the Lord,
he (she) will share at the table of his Sacrifice,
and will call upon God as Father in the midst of the Church.
Now in his (her) name,
and in the spirit of adoption as sons and daughters
which we have all received,
let us pray together as the Lord taught us.

182. And all say together with the celebrant:

Our Father, who art in heaven,
hallowed be thy name;
thy kingdom come,
thy will be done
on earth as it is in heaven.
Give us this day our daily bread,
and forgive us our trespasses,
as we forgive those who trespass against us;
and lead us not into temptation,
but deliver us from evil.

183. Then the celebrant blesses the mother, holding her child in her arms, the father, and all those present, saying:

The Lord God Almighty,
through his Son, born of the Virgin Mary,
brings joy to Christian mothers
as the hope of eternal life shines forth upon their children.
May he graciously bless the mother of this child restored to health,
so that, as she now gives thanks for the gift of her child,
she may always remain united with him (her) in thanksgiving,
in Christ Jesus our Lord.

All:

Amen.

Celebrant:

May the Lord God Almighty,
the giver of life both in heaven and on earth,
bless the father of this child,
so that, together with his wife,
they may, by word and example,
prove to be the first witnesses of the faith to their child,
in Christ Jesus our Lord.

All:

Amen.

Celebrant:

May the Lord God Almighty,
who by water and the Holy Spirit
has given us new birth into eternal life,
abundantly bless his faithful here present,
that always and everywhere they may be active members
    of his people;
and may he bestow his peace on all who are here,
in Christ Jesus our Lord.

All:

Amen.

Celebrant:

**May almighty God bless you,
the Father, and the Son, ✝ and the Holy Spirit.**

All:

Amen.

Celebrant:

Go in peace.

All:

Thanks be to God.

Other optional formulas of blessing. nos. **247–249.**

184. After the blessing, if circumstances suggest, a suitable canticle that expresses paschal joy and thanksgiving or the Canticle of the Blessed Virgin Mary, the **Magnificat**, may be sung by all.

Where it is the custom to bring the baptized infant to the altar of the Blessed Virgin Mary, this custom should appropriately be retained.

185. The Order described above may also be used when other baptized children are brought to the church after other difficulties (e.g., persecution, disagreement between the parents, etc.), which prohibited the celebration of Baptism in church. In these cases, it is for the celebrant to adapt the instructions, readings, intentions of the Prayer of the Faithful, to the situation of the child.

Chapter VII

VARIOUS TEXTS FOR USE IN THE CELEBRATION OF BAPTISM FOR CHILDREN

I. Biblical Readings

Readings from the Old Testament

(Lectionary for Mass, no. 756)

186. *Give us water to drink.*

A reading from the Book of Exodus 17:3–7

In their thirst for water,
    the people grumbled against Moses,
    saying, "Why did you ever make us leave Egypt?
Was it just to have us die here of thirst
    with our children and our livestock?"
So Moses cried out to the LORD,
    "What shall I do with this people?
A little more and they will stone me!"
The LORD answered Moses,
    "Go over there in front of the people,
    along with some of the elders of Israel,
    holding in your hand, as you go,
    the staff with which you struck the river.
I will be standing there in front of you on the rock in Horeb.
Strike the rock, and the water will flow from it
    for the people to drink."
This Moses did, in the presence of the elders of Israel.
The place was called Massah and Meribah,
    because the children of Israel quarreled there
    and tested the LORD, saying,
    "Is the LORD in our midst or not?"

The word of the Lord.

187. *I shall pour clean water upon you to cleanse you from all your impurities.*

A reading from the Book of the Prophet Ezekiel 36:24–28

Thus says the Lord GOD:
I will take you away from among the nations,
    gather you from all the foreign lands,
    and bring you back to your own land.
I will sprinkle clean water upon you
    to cleanse you from all your impurities,
    and from all your idols I will cleanse you.
I will give you a new heart and place a new spirit within you,
    taking from your bodies your stony hearts
    and giving you natural hearts.
I will put my spirit within you and make you live by my statutes,
    careful to observe my decrees.
You shall live in the land I gave your father;
    you shall be my people, and I will be your God.

The word of the Lord.

188. *I saw water flowing from the temple, and all who were touched by it were saved* (see *Roman Missal*, antiphon for blessing and sprinkling holy water during Easter Time).

A reading from the Book of the Prophet Ezekiel 47:1–9, 12

The angel brought me, Ezekiel,
    back to the entrance of the temple of the Lord,
    and I saw water flowing out
    from beneath the threshold of the temple toward the east,
    for the façade of the temple was toward the east;
    the water flowed down from the right side of the temple,
    south of the altar.
He led me outside by the north gate,
    and around to the outer gate facing the east,
    where I saw water trickling from the right side.
Then when he had walked off to the east
    with a measuring cord in his hand,
    he measured off a thousand cubits
    and had me wade through the water,
    which was ankle-deep.

He measured off another thousand
    and once more had me wade through the water,
    which was now knee-deep.
Again he measured off a thousand and had me wade;
    the water was up to my waist.
Once more he measured off a thousand,
    but there was now a river through which I could not wade;
    for the water had risen so high it had become a river
    that could not be crossed except by swimming.
He asked me, "Have you seen this, son of man?"
Then he brought me to the bank of the river, where he had me sit.
Along the bank of the river I saw very many trees on both sides.
He said to me,
    "This water flows into the eastern district down upon
        the Arabah,
    and empties into the sea, the salt waters, which it makes fresh.
Wherever the river flows,
    every sort of living creature that can multiply shall live,
    and there shall be abundant fish,
    for wherever this water comes the sea shall be made fresh.
Along both banks of the river, fruit trees of every kind shall grow;
    their leaves shall not fade, nor their fruit fail.
Every month they shall bear fresh fruit,
    for they shall be watered by the flow from the sanctuary.
Their fruit shall serve for food, and their leaves for medicine."

The word of the Lord.

189. *Buried with him through baptism into death, we too might live in newness of life.*

A reading from the Letter of Saint Paul to the Romans 6:3–5

Brothers and sisters:
Are you unaware that we who were baptized into Christ Jesus
    were baptized into his death?
We were indeed buried with him through baptism into death,
    so that, just as Christ was raised from the dead
    by the glory of the Father,
    we too might live in newness of life.

For if we have grown into union with him through a death like his,
    we shall also be united with him in the resurrection.

The word of the Lord.

190. *To be conformed to the image of his Son.*

A reading from the Letter of Saint Paul to the Romans 8:28–32

Brothers and sisters:
We know that all things work for good for those who love God,
    who are called according to his purpose.
For those he foreknew he also predestined
    to be conformed to the image of his Son,
    so that he might be the firstborn
    among many brothers.
And those he predestined he also called;
    and those he called he also justified;
    and those he justified he also glorified.

What then shall we say to this?
If God is for us, who can be against us?
He who did not spare his own Son
    but handed him over for us all,
    how will he not also give us everything else along with him?

The word of the Lord.

191. *For in one Spirit we were all baptized into one Body.*

A reading from the first Letter of Saint Paul to the Corinthians 12:12–13

Brothers and sisters:
As a body is one though it has many parts,
    and all the parts of the body, though many, are one body,
    so also Christ.
For in one Spirit we were all baptized into one Body,
    whether Jews or Greeks, slaves or free persons,
    and we were all given to drink of one Spirit.

The word of the Lord.

192. *All of you who were baptized into Christ have clothed yourselves with Christ.*

A reading from the Letter of Saint Paul to the Galatians 3:26–28

Brothers and sisters:
Through faith you are all children of God in Christ Jesus.
For all of you who were baptized into Christ
    have clothed yourselves with Christ.
There is neither Jew nor Greek,
    there is neither slave nor free person,
    there is not male and female;
    for you are all one in Christ Jesus.

The word of the Lord.

193. *There is one Lord, one faith, one baptism.*

A reading from the Letter of Saint Paul to the Ephesians   4:1–6

Brothers and sisters:
I, a prisoner for the Lord,
 urge you to live in a manner worthy of the call
  you have received,
 with all humility and gentleness, with patience,
 bearing with one another through love,
 striving to preserve the unity of the spirit
 through the bond of peace:
 one Body and one Spirit,
 as you were also called to the one hope of your call;
 one Lord, one faith, one baptism;
 one God and Father of all,
 who is over all and through all and in all.

The word of the Lord.

194. *You are a chosen race, a royal priesthood.*

A reading from the first Letter of Saint Peter   2:4–5, 9–10

Beloved:
Come to the Lord, a living stone, rejected by human beings
 but chosen and precious in the sight of God,
 and, like living stones,
 let yourselves be built into a spiritual house
 to be a holy priesthood to offer spiritual sacrifices
  acceptable to God through Jesus Christ.

You are "a chosen race, a royal priesthood,
 a holy nation, a people of his own,
 so that you may announce the praises" of him
 who called you out of darkness into his wonderful light.

  Once you were "no people"
   but now you are God's people;
  you "had not received mercy"
   but now you have received mercy.

The word of the Lord.

Responsorial Psalms

(Lectionary for Mass, no. 758)

195. Psalm 23 (22):1–3a, 3b–4, 5, 6

R.   (1) The Lord is my shepherd; there is nothing I shall want.

The LORD is my shepherd;
>   there is nothing I shall want.
Fresh and green are the pastures
>   where he gives me repose.
Near restful waters he leads me;
>   he revives my soul. R.

He guides me along the right path,
>   for the sake of his name.
Though I should walk in the valley of the shadow of death,
>   no evil would I fear, for you are with me.
Your crook and your staff will give me comfort. R.

You have prepared a table before me
>   in the sight of my foes.
My head you have anointed with oil;
>   my cup is overflowing. R.

Surely goodness and mercy shall follow me
>   all the days of my life.
In the LORD's own house shall I dwell
>   for length of days unending. R.

196. Psalm 27 (26):1, 4, 8b–9abcd, 13–14

R.   (1a) The Lord is my light and my salvation.

Or:

R.   (Ephesians 5:14) Wake up and rise from death:
>   Christ will shine upon you!

The LORD is my light and my salvation;
>   whom shall I fear?
The LORD is the stronghold of my life;
>   whom should I dread? R.

There is one thing I ask of the LORD,
    only this do I seek:
to live in the house of the LORD
    all the days of my life,
to gaze on the beauty of the LORD,
    to inquire at his temple. R.

It is your face, O LORD, that I seek;
    hide not your face from me.
Dismiss not your servant in anger;
    you have been my help.
Do not abandon me. R.

I believe I shall see the LORD's goodness
    in the land of the living.
Wait for the LORD; be strong;
    be stouthearted, and wait for the LORD! R.

197. Psalm 34 (33):2–3, 6–7, 8–9, 14–15, 16–17, 18–19

R.   (6a) Look to him, that you may be radiant with joy!

Or:

R.   (9a) Taste and see the goodness of the Lord.

I will bless the LORD at all times;
    praise of him is always in my mouth.
In the LORD my soul shall make its boast;
    the humble shall hear and be glad. R.

Look toward him and be radiant;
    let your faces not be abashed.
This lowly one called; the LORD heard,
    and rescued him from all his distress. R.

The angel of the LORD is encamped
    around those who fear him, to rescue them.
Taste and see that the LORD is good.
    Blessed the man who seeks refuge in him. R.

Guard your tongue from evil,
    and your lips from speaking deceit.
Turn aside from evil and do good.
    Seek after peace, and pursue it. R.

The Lord turns his eyes to the just one,
    and his ears are open to his cry.
The Lord turns his face against the wicked
    to cut off their remembrance from the earth. R.

When the just one cries out, the Lord hears,
    and rescues him in all his distress.
The Lord is close to the brokenhearted;
    those whose spirit is crushed he will save. R.

Alleluia Verse and Verse before the Gospel

(*Lectionary for Mass*, no. 759)

198. John 3:16

God so loved the world that he gave his only-begotten Son,
so that everyone who believes in him might have eternal life.

199. John 8:12

I am the light of the world, says the Lord;
whoever follows me will have the light of life.

200. John 14:6

I am the way and the truth and the life, says the Lord;
no one comes to the Father, except through me.

201. Ephesians 4:5–6

There is one Lord, one faith, one baptism,
one God and the Father of all.

202. Cf. 2 Timothy 1:10

Our Savior Jesus Christ has destroyed death
and brought life to light through the Gospel.

203. 1 Peter 2:9

You are a chosen race, a royal priesthood, a holy nation:
announce the praises of him who called you
out of darkness into his wonderful light.

GOSPEL

(*Lectionary for Mass*, no. 760)

204. *This is the greatest and the first commandment.*

✝ A reading from the holy Gospel according to Matthew   22:35–40

One of the Pharisees, a scholar of the law, tested Jesus by asking,
    "Teacher, which commandment in the law is the greatest?"
He said to him,
    "You shall love the Lord, your God, with all your heart,
    with all your soul, and with all your mind.
This is the greatest and the first commandment.
The second is like it:
    You shall love your neighbor as yourself.
The whole law and the prophets depend on these two
    commandments."

The Gospel of the Lord.

205. *Go, therefore, and make disciples of all nations, baptizing them in the name of the Father, and of the Son, and of the Holy Spirit.*

✝ A reading from the holy Gospel according to Matthew   28:18–20

Jesus said to the Eleven disciples,
"All power in heaven and on earth has been given to me.
Go, therefore, and make disciples of all nations,
    baptizing them in the name of the Father,
    and of the Son, and of the Holy Spirit,
    teaching them to observe all that I have commanded you.
And behold, I am with you always, until the end of the age."

The Gospel of the Lord.

206. *Jesus was baptized in the Jordan by John.*

✝ A reading from the holy Gospel according to Mark   1:9–11

Jesus came from Nazareth of Galilee
    and was baptized in the Jordan by John.
On coming up out of the water he saw the heavens being
       torn open
    and the Spirit, like a dove, descending upon him.

And a voice came from the heavens,
  "You are my beloved Son; with you I am well pleased."

The Gospel of the Lord.

207. *Let the children come to me; do not prevent them.*

✝ **A reading from the holy Gospel according to Mark**   10:13–16

People were bringing children to Jesus that he might touch them,
  but the disciples rebuked them.
When Jesus saw this he became indignant and said to them,
  "Let the children come to me; do not prevent them,
  for the Kingdom of God belongs to such as these.
Amen, I say to you,
  whoever does not accept the Kingdom of God like a child
  will not enter it."
Then he embraced them and blessed them,
  placing his hands on them.

The Gospel of the Lord.

208. Long Form

Hear O Israel! You shall love the Lord, your God, with all your heart.

✝ **A reading from the holy Gospel according to Mark**   12:28b–34

One of the scribes came to Jesus and asked him,
  "Which is the first of all the commandments?"
Jesus replied, "The first is this:
  Hear, O Israel!
  The Lord our God is Lord alone!
You shall love the Lord your God with all your heart,
  with all your soul, with all your mind,
  and with all your strength.
The second is this:
  You shall love your neighbor as yourself.
There is no other commandment greater than these."
The scribe said to him,
  "Well said, teacher. You are right in saying,
  'He is One and there is no other than he.'

And 'to love him with all your heart,
  with all your understanding,
  with all your strength,
  and to love your neighbor as yourself'
  is worth more than all burnt offerings and sacrifices."
And when Jesus saw that he answered with understanding,
  he said to him,
  "You are not far from the Kingdom of God."
And no one dared to ask him any more questions.

The Gospel of the Lord.

Or:

Short Form

Hear O Israel! You shall love the Lord, your God, with all your heart.

✠ A reading from the holy Gospel according to Mark   12:28b–31

One of the scribes came to Jesus and asked him,
  "Which is the first of all the commandments?"
Jesus replied, "The first is this:
  Hear, O Israel!
  The Lord our God is Lord alone!
You shall love the Lord your God with all your heart,
  with all your soul, with all your mind,
  and with all your strength.
The second is this:
  You shall love your neighbor as yourself.
There is no other commandment greater than these."

The Gospel of the Lord.

209. *No one can see the Kingdom of God without being born from above.*

✠ A reading from the holy Gospel according to John   3:1–6

There was a Pharisee named Nicodemus, a ruler of the Jews.
He came to Jesus at night and said to him,
  "Rabbi, we know that you are a teacher who has
    come from God,
  for no one can do these signs that you are doing
  unless God is with him."

Jesus answered and said to him,
>"Amen, amen, I say to you,
>unless one is born from above,
>he cannot see the Kingdom of God."

Nicodemus said to him,
>"How can a man once grown old be born again?
>Surely he cannot reenter his mother's womb and be born again,
>>can he?"

Jesus answered,
>"Amen, amen, I say to you,
>unless one is born of water and Spirit
>he cannot enter the Kingdom of God.

What is born of flesh is flesh
>and what is born of spirit is spirit."

The Gospel of the Lord.

210.   *A spring of water welling up to eternal life.*

✝ A reading from the holy Gospel according to John   4:5–14

Jesus came to a town of Samaria called Sychar,
>near the plot of land that Jacob had given to his son Joseph.

Jacob's well was there.
Jesus, tired from his journey, sat down there at the well.
It was about noon.

A woman of Samaria came to draw water.
Jesus said to her,
>"Give me a drink."

His disciples had gone into the town to buy food.
The Samaritan woman said to him,
>"How can you, a Jew, ask me, a Samaritan woman,
>>for a drink?"

—For Jews use nothing in common with Samaritans.—
Jesus answered and said to her,
>"If you knew the gift of God
>and who is saying to you, 'Give me a drink,'
>you would have asked him
>and he would have given you living water."

The woman said to him,
>"Sir, you do not even have a bucket and the cistern is deep;
>where then can you get this living water?

Are you greater than our father Jacob,
    who gave us this cistern and drank from it himself
    with his children and his flocks?"
Jesus answered and said to her,
    "Everyone who drinks this water will be thirsty again;
    but whoever drinks the water I shall give will never thirst;
    the water I shall give will become in him
    a spring of water welling up to eternal life."

The Gospel of the Lord.

211. *Whoever believes has eternal life.*

✛ **A reading from the holy Gospel according to John**   6:44–47

Jesus said to the crowds:
"No one can come to me unless the Father who sent me draw him,
    and I will raise him on the last day.
It is written in the prophets:
    They shall all be taught by God.
Everyone who listens to my Father and learns from him
        comes to me.
Not that anyone has seen the Father
    except the one who is from God;
    he has seen the Father.
Amen, amen, I say to you,
    whoever believes has eternal life."

The Gospel of the Lord.

212. *Rivers of living water will flow.*

✛ **A reading from the holy Gospel according to John**   7:37b–39a

Jesus stood up and exclaimed,
    "Let anyone who thirsts come to me and drink.
Whoever believes in me, as Scripture says:
    Rivers of living water will flow from within him."
He said this in reference to the Spirit
    that those who came to believe in him were to receive.

The Gospel of the Lord.

213. *So he went and washed and came back able to see.*

✠ A reading from the holy Gospel according to John 9:1–7

As Jesus passed by he saw a man blind from birth.
His disciples asked him,
> "Rabbi, who sinned, this man or his parents,
> that he was born blind?"
Jesus answered,
> "Neither he nor his parents sinned;
> it is so that the works of God might be made visible
> > through him.
We have to do the works of the one who sent me while it is day.
Night is coming when no one can work.
While I am in the world, I am the light of the world."
When he had said this, he spat on the ground
> and made clay with the saliva,
> and smeared the clay on his eyes, and said to him,
> "Go wash in the Pool of Siloam" (which means Sent).
So he went and washed, and came back able to see.

The Gospel of the Lord.

214. *Whoever remains in me and I in him will bear much fruit.*

✠ A reading from the holy Gospel according to John 15:1–11

Jesus said to his disciples:
"I am the true vine, and my Father is the vine grower.
He takes away every branch in me that does not bear fruit,
> and everyone that does he prunes so that it bears more fruit.
You are already pruned because of the word that I spoke to you.
Remain in me, as I remain in you.
Just as a branch cannot bear fruit on its own
> unless it remains on the vine,
> so neither can you unless you remain in me.
I am the vine, you are the branches.
Whoever remains in me and I in him will bear much fruit,
> because without me you can do nothing.
Anyone who does not remain in me
> will be thrown out like a branch and wither;
> people will gather them and throw them into a fire
> and they will be burned.

If you remain in me and my words remain in you,
    ask for whatever you want and it will be done for you.
By this is my Father glorified,
    that you bear much fruit and become my disciples.
As the Father loves me, so I also love you.
Remain in my love.
If you keep my commandments, you will remain in my love,
    just as I have kept my Father's commandments
    and remain in his love.

"I have told you this so that my joy may be in you
    and your joy may be complete."

The Gospel of the Lord.

215. *One soldier thrust his lance into his side, and immediately Blood and water flowed out.*

✠ A reading from the holy Gospel according to John   19:31–35

Since it was preparation day,
    in order that the bodies might not remain on the cross
        on the sabbath,
    for the sabbath day of that week was a solemn one,
    the Jews asked Pilate that their legs be broken
    and they be taken down.
So the soldiers came and broke the legs of the first
    and then of the other one who was crucified with Jesus.
But when they came to Jesus and saw that he was already dead,
    they did not break his legs,
    but one soldier thrust his lance into his side,
    and immediately Blood and water flowed out.
An eyewitness has testified, and his testimony is true;
    he knows that he is speaking the truth,
    so that you also may come to believe.

The Gospel of the Lord.

II. Formulas for the Prayer of the Faithful

From all the formulas which are set out either here or in the Order of Baptism, one or another may be used. It is, however, permissible to choose elements from each, or to insert new ones, so that the prayer may be more suitable, and most importantly take account of the special needs of the families. But the prayer is always concluded with the invocation of the Saints.

1

216. Cf. above, in the "Order of Baptism for Several Children," no. 47.

2

217.

We are called by the Lord to be a royal priesthood,
a holy nation and a people he has gained for his own possession.
And so, let us invoke the mercy of almighty God
for these children, about to receive the grace of Baptism,
and for their parents, godparents, and all the baptized.

That you would join these children to the Church
    through Baptism:

R.   Lord, we ask you, hear our prayer.

That, signed with the Sign of the Cross,
they may openly profess on all the pathways of life
that Christ is the Son of God:

R.   Lord, we ask you, hear our prayer.

That, buried with Christ through Baptism into his Death,
they may also share in his Resurrection:

R.   Lord, we ask you, hear our prayer.

That, instructed by the word and example of their parents
    and godparents,
they may grow to be active members of the Church:

R.   Lord, we ask you, hear our prayer.

That the grace of Baptism may be renewed
in all those gathered here:

R.   Lord, we ask you, hear our prayer.

That all Christ's disciples, baptized into one body,
may remain together always in faith and love.

R.   Lord, we ask you, hear our prayer.

The invocations of the Saints follow.

3   218.

Dear brothers and sisters,
let us invoke the mercy of our Lord Jesus Christ
for these children about to receive the grace of Baptism,
and for their parents, godparents, and all the baptized.

That through Baptism these children may receive adoption
        as sons and daughters,
let us pray to the Lord.

R.   Lord, we ask you, hear our prayer.

That, as branches grafted into the true vine,
these disciples of Christ may come to perfection in their faith,
let us pray to the Lord.

R.   Lord, we ask you, hear our prayer.

That, obedient to Christ's commandments,
they may always remain in his love
and boldly proclaim the Gospel to others,
let us pray to the Lord.

R.   Lord, we ask you, hear our prayer.

That, justified by the grace of Christ the Savior,
they may obtain an eternal inheritance,
let us pray to the Lord.

R.   Lord, we ask you, hear our prayer.

That the parents and godparents may instruct these children
in the knowledge and love of God,
let us pray to the Lord.

R.   Lord, we ask you, hear our prayer.

That all people may share in the rebirth that comes from Baptism,
let us pray to the Lord.

R.   Lord, we ask you, hear our prayer.

The invocations of the Saints follow.

4   219.

We are called by the Lord to be a royal priesthood,
a holy nation and a people he has gained for his own possession.
And so, let us invoke the mercy of almighty God
for these children, about to receive the grace of Baptism,
and for their parents, godparents, and all the baptized.

That through Baptism, these children may be made sons and
        daughters of adoption,
in whom God is well pleased,
let us pray to the Lord.

R.   Lord, we ask you, hear our prayer.

That born again of water and the Holy Spirit,
and living always in that Spirit,
they may show forth the new life to others,
let us pray to the Lord.

R.   Lord, we ask you, hear our prayer.

That they may be able to overcome
the snares of the devil and the allurements of vice,
let us pray to the Lord.

R.   Lord, we ask you, hear our prayer.

That they may love the Lord with all their heart, soul, mind,
        and strength,
and their neighbor as themselves,
let us pray to the Lord.

R.   Lord, we ask you, hear our prayer.

That we who are present will offer the witness of our faith
        to these children,
let us pray to the Lord.

R.   Lord, we ask you, hear our prayer.

That always and everywhere,
all the Christian faithful may manifest in their conduct
the Sign of the Cross received in Baptism,
let us pray to the Lord.

R.   Lord, we ask you, hear our prayer.

The invocations of the Saints follow.

5   220.

Let us implore the mercy of Christ
for these children,
and for their parents, godparents, and all the baptized.

That they may be born again of water and the Holy Spirit
     into eternal life:

R.   Lord, we ask you, hear our prayer.

That they may be made active members of your holy Church:

R.   Lord, we ask you, hear our prayer.

That they may hear your holy Gospel, abide by it,
     and bear witness to it:

R.   Lord, we ask you, hear our prayer.

That they may come joyfully to the table of your Sacrifice:

R.   Lord, we ask you, hear our prayer.

That they may love the Lord God and their neighbor,
as you have taught:

R.   Lord, we ask you, hear our prayer.

That, instructed by the word and example of Christians,
they may grow in holiness and wisdom:

R.   Lord, we ask you, hear our prayer.

That all your disciples may live always united in faith and love:

R.   Lord, we ask you, hear our prayer.

The invocations of the Saints follow.

II-A. Another Litany of the Saints

220A.

Holy Mary, Mother of God,	pray for us.
Saint Michael,	pray for us.
Holy Angels of God,	pray for us.
Saint John the Baptist,	pray for us.
Saint Joseph,	pray for us.
Saint Peter and Saint Paul,	pray for us.
Saint Andrew,	pray for us.
Saint John,	pray for us.
Saint Mary Magdalene,	pray for us.
Saint Stephen,	pray for us.
Saint Ignatius of Antioch,	pray for us.
Saint Lawrence,	pray for us.
Saint Perpetua and Saint Felicity,	pray for us.
Saint Agnes,	pray for us.
Saint Gregory,	pray for us.
Saint Augustine,	pray for us.
Saint Athanasius,	pray for us.
Saint Basil,	pray for us.
Saint Martin,	pray for us.
Saint Benedict,	pray for us.
Saint Francis and Saint Dominic,	pray for us.
Saint Francis Xavier,	pray for us.
Saint John Vianney,	pray for us.
Saint Catherine of Siena,	pray for us.
Saint Teresa of Jesus,	pray for us.

It is good to add the names of other Saints, especially those who are Patron Saints of the children or of the church or of the place. Then the Litany concludes:

All holy men and women, Saints of God,	pray for us.

III. Another Prayer of Exorcism

221.

Lord God Almighty,
who sent your Only Begotten Son
to endow humankind,
imprisoned in slavery to sin,
with the freedom of your sons and daughters,
we pray most humbly for these children,
whom you know will experience the allurements of this world,
and will fight against the snares of the devil:
by the power of the Passion and Resurrection of your Son
deliver them now from the stain of Original Sin,
strengthen them with the grace of Christ,
and guard them always on their journey through life.
Through Christ our Lord.

R.   Amen.

IV. Blessing of Water and Invocation of God over the Water

1   222. Cf. the formula in the "Order of Baptism for Several Children," no. 54.

2   223.

Celebrant:

Blessed are you, God the Father almighty,
for you have created water to cleanse and give life.

All:

Blessed be God.

(Or another suitable acclamation of the people.)

Celebrant:

Blessed are you, God the Only Begotten Son, Jesus Christ,
for you poured forth water with blood from your side,
so that from your Death and Resurrection the Church
might be born.

All:

Blessed be God.

Celebrant:

Blessed are you, God the Holy Spirit,
for you anointed Christ at his baptism in the waters of the Jordan,
that we might all be baptized into you.

All:

Blessed be God.

Celebrant:

* Draw near to us, Lord, the one Father,
and sanctify this water you have created,
that those baptized in it may be washed clean of sin
and be born again to the life of your adopted children.

All:

Hear us, O Lord.

(Or another suitable invocation of the people.)

Celebrant:

Sanctify this water you have created,
that those baptized through it into Christ's Death and Resurrection,
may be conformed to the image of your Son.

All:

Hear us, O Lord.

The celebrant touches the water with his right hand and continues:

Sanctify this water you have created,
that those you have chosen may be born again by the Holy Spirit,
and have a portion among your holy people.

All:

Hear us, O Lord.

---

* When there is baptismal water already blessed at hand, omitting the
invocation **Draw near to us** and those which follow, the celebrant says:

By the mystery of this blessed water,
graciously lead to spiritual rebirth your servants (N. and N.),
whom you have called to this cleansing in the faith of the Church,
that they may have eternal life.
Through Christ our Lord.

All:

Amen.

---

3   224.

Celebrant:

Most merciful Father,
from the font of Baptism,
you have made the new life of your children
well up within us.

All:

Blessed be God.

(Or another suitable acclamation of the people.)

Celebrant:

**You have been pleased to unite
by water and the Holy Spirit
all the baptized into one people in your Son Jesus Christ.**

All:

Blessed be God.

Celebrant:

**You free us by the Spirit of your love,
whom you pour into our hearts,
so that we may delight in your peace.**

All:

Blessed be God.

Celebrant:

**You choose the baptized,
that they may joyfully proclaim to all the nations
the Gospel of your Christ.**

All:

Blessed be God.

Celebrant:

*** Be pleased now to bless ✝ this water,
by which your servants (N. and N.) are to be baptized,
for you have called them to this cleansing water of rebirth
in the faith of the Church,
that they may have eternal life.
Through Christ our Lord.**

All:

Amen.

> * When there is baptismal water already blessed at hand, omitting the
> invocation Be pleased now to bless this water, the celebrant says:
>
> **By the mystery of this blessed water,**
> **graciously lead to spiritual rebirth your servants (N. and N.),**
> **whom you have called to this cleansing in the faith of the Church,**
> **that they may have eternal life.**
> **Through Christ our Lord.**
>
> All:
>
> Amen.

V. Acclamations, Hymns, and Chants

Acclamations Taken from Sacred Scripture

225.

Who is like you, O Lord, among the strong?
Who is like you, magnificent in holiness,
worthy of awe and praise, worker of wonders!   (Ex 15:11)

226.

God is light and in him there is no darkness at all.   (1 Jn 1:5)

227.

God is love and whoever abides in love abides in God.   (1 Jn 4:16)

228.

There is one God and Father of all,
who is over all and through all and in us all.   (Eph 4:6)

229.

Look toward the Lord and be radiant;
let your faces not be abashed.   (Ps 33:6)

230.

Blessed be God, who chose you in Christ.   (Cf. Eph 1:3–4)

231.

You are God's work of art, created in Christ Jesus.   (Eph 2:10)

232.

You are now God's children, my beloved,
and what you will be has not yet been revealed.   (1 Jn 3:2)

233.

What great love the Father has given you,
that you should be called and be children of God.   (1 Jn 3:1)

234.

Blessed are they who wash their robes
in the blood of the Lamb!   (Rev 22:14)

235.

All of you are one in Christ Jesus.   (Gal 3:28)

236.

Be imitators of God and walk in love,
as Christ has loved us.   (Eph 5:1–2)

HYMNS IN THE STYLE OF THE NEW TESTAMENT

237.

Blessed be the God and Father of our Lord Jesus Christ,
who in his great mercy has given us new birth into a living hope
through the Resurrection of Jesus Christ from the dead,
into an inheritance that will not perish,
preserved for us in heaven,
for the salvation to be revealed in the last time!   (1 Pt 1:3–5)

238.

Great is the mystery of our religion,
known before the foundation of the world,
revealed in these last days:
Christ Jesus,
having suffered and been put to death in the flesh,
brought to life in the Spirit,
proclaimed to the nations,
believed in throughout the world:
he entered into heaven,
bestowing gifts on the human race,
and was raised in glory above all the heavens,
so that he might fill all things, alleluia.   (Cf. 1 Tim 3:16)

CHANTS SELECTED FROM ANTIQUITY AND FROM THE LITURGIES

239.

We believe in you, O Christ:
pour your light into our hearts
to make us children of light!

240.

We come to you, O Lord:
fill our souls with your life,
that in you we may become
children of adoption.

241.

From your side, O Christ,
bursts forth a spring of water,
by which the squalor of the world is washed away
and life is made new again.

242.

The voice of the Father sounds above the waters,
the glory of the Son shines brightly forth,
and the love of the Holy Spirit gives life.

243.

Holy Church, stretch out your hands
to welcome those brought to new birth from the waters
by the Holy Spirit of God.

244.

Rejoice, you newly baptized,
chosen vessels of the Kingdom,
buried together with Christ in death,
born again of Christ by faith.

245.

This is the font of life
that washes all the world,
flowing from Christ's wounded side.
Hope for the Kingdom of Heaven,
all you reborn in this font.

VI. Formulas of Final Blessing

1   246. Cf. no. 70 in the "Order of Baptism for Several Children."

2   247.

Celebrant:

**May the Lord God Almighty,
who through the birth in time of his Son
has flooded the world with joy,
bless these newly baptized children,
that they may be fully conformed to Christ.**

All:

Amen.

Celebrant:

May the Lord God Almighty,
who bestows life on earth and in heaven,
graciously bless these fathers and mothers,
so that, as they now give thanks for the gift of their children,
they may always remain united with them in thanksgiving.

All:

Amen.

Celebrant:

May the Lord God Almighty,
who by water and the Holy Spirit
has given us new birth into eternal life,
abundantly bless these faithful here present,
that always and everywhere they may be active members
    of his people;
and may he bestow his peace on all who are here.

All:

Amen.

Celebrant:

May almighty God bless you,
the Father, and the Son, ✝ and the Holy Spirit.

All:

Amen.

Celebrant:

Go in peace.

All:

Thanks be to God.

3   248.

Celebrant:

May God, the author of life and love,
who has given mothers a generous heart to embrace their children,
look upon these mothers and bless them,
so that, as they give thanks for the gift of their children,
they may rejoice in their love, their growth, and their virtue.

All:

Amen.

Celebrant:

May God, the origin and model of all fatherhood,
also accompany with his favor the fathers of these children,
so that, by the example of their conduct,
they may lead them to the maturity of Christian life.

All:

Amen.

Celebrant:

May God, the lover of all,
look mercifully now on the relatives and friends gathered here,
that he may guard them from evil
and bestow on them abundant peace.

All:

Amen.

Celebrant:

May almighty God bless you,
the Father, and the Son, ✝ and the Holy Spirit.

All:

Amen.

Celebrant:

Go in peace.

All:

Thanks be to God.

4   249.

Celebrant:

**Brothers and sisters,
we commend you to the mercies and grace
of God the almighty Father,
of his Only Begotten Son,
and of the Holy Spirit.
May he guard your life,
so that, walking in the light of faith,
you may come to the good things that are promised
and we together with you.**

All:

Amen.

Celebrant:

**May almighty God bless you,
the Father, and the Son, ✝ and the Holy Spirit.**

All:

Amen.

Celebrant:

Go in peace.

All:

Thanks be to God.

Appendix

ORDER OF BAPTISM OF CHILDREN WITHIN MASS

INTRODUCTION

250. To illustrate the paschal character of Baptism, it is recommended that the Sacrament be celebrated at the Easter Vigil or on a Sunday, when the Church commemorates the Resurrection of the Lord. Furthermore, on a Sunday, Baptism may be celebrated also within Mass, so that the whole community may be able to take part in the rite and so that the connection between Baptism and the Most Holy Eucharist may stand out more clearly. Nevertheless, this should not happen too often.[1]

251. This ritual set out in this Appendix is provided to assist Priests who wish to celebrate Baptism within Mass, and is based on the instructions found in the Introduction of the *Order of Baptism of Children*, nos. 29–30. The celebration of Baptism within Mass is arranged as follows:

1. The rite of receiving the children is done at the beginning of the Mass, and the Greeting and Penitential Act are omitted. When prescribed, the *Gloria in excelsis* (*Glory to God in the highest*) is sung or said.
2. The options for the Readings are described in nos. 269 and 307, below. The Homily is based on the sacred text, but should take into consideration the Baptism being celebrated.
3. The Creed is not said, because its place is taken by the profession of faith, which is made by the entire community before the Baptism.
4. The Universal Prayer (Prayer of the Faithful) is taken from those in the *Order of Baptism*. At the end, however, before the invocation of the Saints, petitions are added for the universal Church and for the needs of the world.
5. The celebration of Baptism continues with the prayer of exorcism and the anointing and the other rites described in the *Order of Baptism*.
6. When the celebration of Baptism is concluded, the Mass continues as usual with the Offertory.
7. For imparting the blessing at the end of Mass, the Priest may use one of the formulas which are given for the rite of Baptism.

---

1. Cf. *Order of Baptism of Children* (OBC), Introduction, no. 9.

252. When Baptism is conferred during Sunday Mass, the Mass of the day is said or, during the Sundays of Christmas Time or of Ordinary Time, or on weekdays, the Ritual Mass for the Conferral of Baptism is said.[2] However, while Baptism may still be conferred during Mass, the Ritual Mass is prohibited on Sundays of Advent, Lent, and Easter, on Solemnities, on the days within the Octave of Easter, on the Commemoration of All the Faithful Departed (All Souls' Day), on Ash Wednesday, and during Holy Week.[3]

253. When the Baptism of children is celebrated during the Easter Vigil, the service is arranged as described in the Introduction of the *Order of Baptism of Children*, no. 28.

254. In celebrating Baptism, the rites that are to be performed outside the baptistery should take place in the different areas of the church that best suit both the number of those present and the various parts of the baptismal liturgy. When celebrated during Mass, insofar as possible, the rites should be arranged so that they may be seen and heard by all the faithful. Therefore, it is also permitted to choose other suitable locations within the church for those parts that are normally celebrated inside the baptistery, if the chapel of the baptistery is unable to accommodate all the children with their parents and godparents, or all of those present.[4]

255. It is for the father and mother, together with the godparents, to present the child to the Church for Baptism.

256. If there are very many children to be baptized, and there are several Priests or Deacons present, these may assist the celebrant in performing those rites that are indicated in the text.

---

2. Cf. OBC, Introduction, nos. 29 and 30.

3. Cf. *General Instruction of the Roman Missal*, no. 372.

4. Cf. *Christian Initiation*, General Introduction, no. 26.

OUTLINE OF THE RITE

THE INTRODUCTORY RITES

Rite of Receiving the Children
Procession to the Altar
(Glory to God in the Highest)
Collect Prayer

THE LITURGY OF THE WORD

Biblical Readings and Homily
Universal Prayer (Prayer of the Faithful)
    and Litany
Prayer of Exorcism
    (and Anointing before Baptism)
Procession to the Place of Baptism

CELEBRATION OF BAPTISM

Blessing of Water and Invocation of God
    over the Water
Renunciation of Sin and Profession of Faith
Baptism

EXPLANATORY RITES

Anointing after Baptism
Clothing with a White Garment
Handing On of a Lighted Candle
("Ephphatha")

THE LITURGY OF THE EUCHARIST

THE CONCLUDING RITES

Blessing and Dismissal

ORDER OF BAPTISM FOR SEVERAL CHILDREN WITHIN MASS

THE INTRODUCTORY RITES

RITE OF RECEIVING THE CHILDREN

257. When the people are gathered, they sing the Entrance Chant or a suitable Psalm or hymn, if circumstances allow. Meanwhile, the Priest celebrant, wearing vestments with the color proper to the day or the liturgical time, or with the color white or a festive color on days when Ritual Masses are permitted, goes with the ministers to the door of the church, or to that part of the church where the parents and godparents are gathered with those to be baptized.

258. When the Entrance Chant is concluded, the Priest and the faithful, standing, sign themselves with the Sign of the Cross, while the Priest says:

In the name of the Father, and of the Son, and of the Holy Spirit.

The people reply:

Amen.

259. The Greeting and Penitential Act from the *Roman Missal* are omitted. Instead, the celebrant greets those present, especially the parents and godparents, recalling in a few words the joy with which the parents received their children as a gift from God, who is the source of all life and who now wishes to bestow his own life on them. He may use these or similar words:

Dear parents and godparents:
Your families have experienced great joy at the birth
of your children,
and the Church shares your happiness.
Today this joy has brought you to the Church
to give thanks to God for the gift of your children
and to celebrate a new birth in the waters of Baptism.

This community rejoices with you,
for today the number of those baptized in Christ will be increased,
and we offer you our support in raising your children
in the practice of the faith.
Therefore, brothers and sisters,
let us now prepare ourselves to participate in this celebration,
listening to God's Word, praying for these children
    and their families,
and renewing our commitment to the Lord and to his people.

260. The celebrant first asks the parents of each child:

What name do you give (or: have you given) your child?

Parents:

N.

Celebrant:

What do you ask of God's Church for N.?

Parents:

Baptism.

The celebrant may use other words in this dialogue.

The first reply may be given by another person if, according to local custom, this person has the right to give the name.

In the second reply, the parents may use other words: e.g., Faith or The grace of Christ or Entry into the Church or Eternal life.

261. If there are many to be baptized, the celebrant may ask all the parents at once for the names of their children:

What name do you give (or: have you given) your child?

Each family replies in turn. The second question may be put to all at once in the plural.

Celebrant:

What do you ask of God's Church for your children?

All:

Baptism.

262. Then the celebrant addresses the parents in these or similar words:

**In asking for Baptism for your children,
you are undertaking the responsibility
of raising them in the faith,
so that, keeping God's commandments,
they may love the Lord and their neighbor as Christ has taught us.
Do you understand this responsibility?**

Parents:

We do.

This reply is given by each family individually; but if the number of children to be baptized is very large, the reply may be given by all together.

263. Then turning to the godparents, the celebrant asks in these or similar words:

Are you ready to help the parents of these children in their duty?

All the godparents together:

We are.

264. Then the celebrant continues, saying:

N. and N. (or: **Dear children**),
the Church of God receives you with great joy.
In her name I sign you with the Sign of the Cross
 of Christ our Savior;
then, after me, your parents (and godparents) will do the same.

And, without saying anything, he signs each of the children on the forehead. Afterwards he invites the parents, and if it seems appropriate, the godparents, to do the same.

265. The procession to the altar then takes place in the customary manner. If circumstances permit, the procession takes place with singing (e.g., Psalm 85 [84]:7–9ab).

Psalm 85 (84):7–9ab

Will you not restore again our life,
 that your people may rejoice in you?
Show us, O Lord, your mercy,
 and grant us your salvation.
I will hear what the Lord God speaks;
 he speaks of peace for his people and his faithful.

266. The Priest approaches the altar with the ministers. When he has arrived at the altar, after making a profound bow with the ministers, the Priest venerates the altar with a kiss and, if appropriate, incenses the cross and the altar. Then, with the ministers, he goes to the chair.

GLORY TO GOD IN THE HIGHEST

267. Then, when it is prescribed, this hymn is either sung or said:

Glory to God in the highest,
and on earth peace to people of good will.

We praise you,
we bless you,
we adore you,
we glorify you,
we give you thanks for your great glory,
Lord God, heavenly King,
O God, almighty Father.

Lord Jesus Christ, Only Begotten Son,
Lord God, Lamb of God, Son of the Father,
you take away the sins of the world,
    have mercy on us;
you take away the sins of the world,
receive our prayer;
you are seated at the right hand of the Father,
    have mercy on us.

For you alone are the Holy One,
you alone are the Lord,
you alone are the Most High,
Jesus Christ,
with the Holy Spirit,
in the glory of God the Father.
Amen.

COLLECT PRAYER

268. When this hymn is concluded, the Priest, with hands joined, says:

Let us pray.

And all pray in silence with the Priest for a while. Then the Priest, with hands extended, says the Collect prayer. The Collect of the day is used, but on days when Ritual Masses are permitted, one of the following prayers is said:

**O God, who bring us to participate in the mystery
of the Passion and Resurrection of your Son,
grant, we pray,
that, strengthened by the spirit of adoption as your children,
we may always walk in newness of life.
Through our Lord Jesus Christ, your Son,
who lives and reigns with you in the unity of the Holy Spirit,
one God, for ever and ever.**

All:

Amen.

Or:

O God, who bring us to rebirth by the word of life,
grant that, accepting it with a sincere heart,
we may be eager to live by the truth
and may bear abundant fruits of fraternal charity.
Through our Lord Jesus Christ, your Son,
who lives and reigns with you in the unity of the Holy Spirit,
one God, for ever and ever.

All:

Amen.

THE LITURGY OF THE WORD

BIBLICAL READINGS AND HOMILY

269. The celebrant invites the parents, godparents, and others present to take part in the Liturgy of the Word. The children to be baptized may be taken to a separate place, until the celebration of the Word of God is completed.

The Liturgy of the Word is celebrated in the usual manner. At Sunday Masses, the readings are taken from the Mass of the day. During Christmas Time and Ordinary Time, and at weekday Masses, they may also be taken from those which are given in the *Lectionary for Mass* (nos. 756–760) or in this Order (nos. 44, 186–215).

When a Ritual Mass is not permitted, one of the readings may be taken from the texts provided for the Baptism of children, having due regard for the pastoral needs of the faithful and the character of the liturgical day.

270. After the Readings, the celebrant preaches the Homily, which is based on the sacred text, but should take into consideration the Baptism being celebrated.

271. After the Homily, it is recommended that there be a period of silence in which all, invited by the celebrant, pray in their hearts.

The Creed is not said, because its place is taken by the profession of faith, which is made by the entire community before the Baptism.

UNIVERSAL PRAYER (PRAYER OF THE FAITHFUL)

272. The Universal Prayer (Prayer of the Faithful) is taken from those in the *Order of Baptism*. At the end, however, before the invocation of the Saints, petitions are added for the universal Church and for the needs of the world.

Celebrant:

Dear brothers and sisters,
let us invoke the mercy of our Lord Jesus Christ
for these children about to receive the grace of Baptism,
and for their parents, godparents, and all the baptized.

Lector:

Give these children new birth in Baptism
through the radiant divine mystery of your Death and Resurrection,
and join them to your holy Church:

All:

Lord, we ask you, hear our prayer.

Lector:

Make them faithful disciples and witnesses to your Gospel
through Baptism and Confirmation:

All:

Lord, we ask you, hear our prayer.

Lector:

Lead them through holiness of life
to the joys of the heavenly Kingdom:

All:

Lord, we ask you, hear our prayer.

Lector:

Make their parents and godparents
a shining example of the faith to these children:

All:

Lord, we ask you, hear our prayer.

Lector:

Keep their families always in your love:

All:

Lord, we ask you, hear our prayer.

Lector:

Renew the grace of Baptism in each of us:

All:

Lord, we ask you, hear our prayer.

Other optional formulas, nos. 217–220.

273. Afterwards, the celebrant invites those present to invoke the aid of the Saints (if the circumstances require, the children are brought back into the church):

Holy Mary, Mother of God,	pray for us.
Saint John the Baptist,	pray for us.
Saint Joseph,	pray for us.
Saint Peter and Saint Paul,	pray for us.

It is good to add the names of other Saints, especially those who are Patron Saints of the children or of the church or of the place. Then the Litany concludes:

All holy men and women, Saints of God,	pray for us.

Optional extended form of the Litany, no. 220A.

274. After the invocations, the celebrant says:

Almighty ever-living God,
who sent your Son into the world
to drive out from us the power of Satan, the spirit of evil,
and bring the human race, rescued from darkness,
into the marvelous Kingdom of your light:
we humbly beseech you
to free these children from Original Sin,
to make them the temple of your glory,
and to grant that your Holy Spirit may dwell in them.
Through Christ our Lord.

All:

Amen.

Another formula for the Prayer of Exorcism, no. 221.

275. The celebrant continues:

May the strength of Christ the Savior protect you.
As a sign of this we anoint you with the oil of salvation
in the same Christ our Lord,
who lives and reigns for ever and ever.

All:

Amen.

Those to be baptized are anointed one at a time on the breast with the Oil of Catechumens. If there are many children, it is permitted to make use of several ministers.

276. In the United States, if, for serious reasons, the celebrant judges it pastorally necessary or desirable, the Anointing before Baptism may be omitted. In that case, the celebrant says only once:

May the strength of Christ the Savior protect you;
who lives and reigns for ever and ever.

All:

Amen.

And immediately, without saying anything, he lays his hand on each of the children.

277. Then, if the baptistery is outside the church or out of sight of the faithful, there is a procession to it.

But if it is located within view of the congregation, the celebrant, parents, and godparents go there with the children and the others remain in their places.

If the baptistery cannot accommodate all those present, it is permitted to celebrate the Baptism in a more suitable place, with the parents and godparents coming forward at the appropriate time.

Meanwhile, if it can be done with dignity, a suitable liturgical song is sung, e.g., Psalm 23 (22).

Psalm 23 (22)

The LORD is my shepherd;
    there is nothing I shall want.
Fresh and green are the pastures
    where he gives me repose.
Near restful waters he leads me;
    he revives my soul.

He guides me along the right path,
    for the sake of his name.
Though I should walk in the valley of the shadow of death,
    no evil would I fear, for you are with me.
Your crook and your staff will give me comfort.

You have prepared a table before me
    in the sight of my foes.
My head you have anointed with oil;
    my cup is overflowing.

Surely goodness and mercy shall follow me
    all the days of my life.
In the LORD's own house shall I dwell
    for length of days unending.

Celebration of Baptism

278. When they have come to the font, the celebrant briefly reminds those present of the wonderful plan of God, who willed to sanctify the human soul and body through water. He may do this in these or similar words:

Let us pray, dear brothers and sisters,
that the Lord God Almighty may bestow new life on these children
by water and the Holy Spirit.

Or:

Dear brothers and sisters,
you know that God graciously bestows
his abundant life through the sacrament of water
on those who believe.
Let us then raise our minds to him,
and with one heart pray
that he may be pleased to pour out his grace from this font
upon these chosen ones.

Blessing of Water and Invocation of God over the Water

279. Then, turning to the font, the celebrant says the following Blessing (outside Easter Time):

O God, who by invisible power
accomplish a wondrous effect
through sacramental signs
and who in many ways have prepared water, your creation,
to show forth the grace of Baptism;

O God, whose Spirit
in the first moments of the world's creation
hovered over the waters,
so that the very substance of water
would even then take to itself the power to sanctify;

O God, who by the outpouring of the flood
foreshadowed regeneration,
so that from the mystery of one and the same element of water
would come an end to vice and a beginning of virtue;

O God, who caused the children of Abraham
to pass dry-shod through the Red Sea,
so that the chosen people,
set free from slavery to Pharaoh,
would prefigure the people of the baptized;

O God, whose Son,
baptized by John in the waters of the Jordan,
was anointed with the Holy Spirit,
and, as he hung upon the Cross,
gave forth water from his side along with blood,
and after his Resurrection, commanded his disciples:
"Go forth, teach all nations, baptizing them
in the name of the Father and of the Son and of the Holy Spirit,"
look now, we pray, upon the face of your Church
and graciously unseal for her the fountain of Baptism.

May this water receive by the Holy Spirit
the grace of your Only Begotten Son,
so that human nature, created in your image
and washed clean through the Sacrament of Baptism
from all the squalor of the life of old,
may be found worthy to rise to the life of newborn children
through water and the Holy Spirit.

The celebrant touches the water with his right hand and continues:

May the power of the Holy Spirit,
O Lord, we pray,
come down through your Son
into the fullness of this font,
so that all who have been buried with Christ
by Baptism into death
may rise again to life with him.
Who lives and reigns for ever and ever.

All:

Amen.

Other optional formulas, nos. 223–224.

280. During Easter Time, however, if the baptismal water has been consecrated at the Easter Vigil, so that the Baptism may not lack the element of thanksgiving and petition, the blessing and invocation of God over the water takes place in accordance with the formulas found in nos. 223–224, using the textual variation given at the end of these same formulas.

RENUNCIATION OF SIN AND PROFESSION OF FAITH

281. The celebrant instructs the parents and godparents in these words:

Dear parents and godparents:
through the Sacrament of Baptism
the children you have presented
are about to receive from the love of God
new life by water and the Holy Spirit.

For your part, you must strive to bring them up in the faith,
so that this divine life may be preserved from the contagion of sin,
and may grow in them day by day.

If your faith makes you ready to accept this responsibility,
then, mindful of your own Baptism,
renounce sin and profess faith in Christ Jesus,
the faith of the Church,
in which children are baptized.

The celebrant also invites the entire community to join in the renunciation of sin and profession of faith.

282. Then the celebrant questions them:

Do you renounce Satan?

Parents, godparents, and all present:

I do.

Celebrant:

And all his works?

Parents, godparents, and all present:

I do.

Celebrant:

And all his empty show?

Parents, godparents, and all present:

I do.

Or:

Celebrant:

**Do you renounce sin,
so as to live in the freedom of the children of God?**

Parents, godparents, and all present:

I do.

Celebrant:

**Do you renounce the lure of evil,
so that sin may have no mastery over you?**

Parents, godparents, and all present:

I do.

Celebrant:

**Do you renounce Satan,
the author and prince of sin?**

Parents, godparents, and all present:

I do.

In the United States, if the occasion requires, this second formula may
be adapted with more precision by the Diocesan Bishop, especially
when it is necessary that the parents and godparents should renounce
superstitions, divinations, and magical arts practiced with reference to
the children.

283. Next, the celebrant elicits the threefold profession of faith by the parents and godparents, and by the entire community, saying:

Do you believe in God,
the Father almighty,
Creator of heaven and earth?

Parents, godparents, and all present:

I do.

Celebrant:

Do you believe in Jesus Christ, his only Son, our Lord,
who was born of the Virgin Mary,
suffered death and was buried,
rose again from the dead
and is seated at the right hand of the Father?

Parents, godparents, and all present:

I do.

Celebrant:

Do you believe in the Holy Spirit,
the holy catholic Church,
the communion of saints,
the forgiveness of sins,
the resurrection of the body,
and life everlasting?

Parents, godparents, and all present:

I do.

284. The celebrant, together with the community, gives assent to this profession of faith, saying:

This is our faith. This is the faith of the Church.
We are proud to profess it in Christ Jesus our Lord.

All:

Amen.

Another formula may be substituted, if circumstances suggest. Or a suitable liturgical song, by which the community expresses its faith with one voice, may be sung.

285. The celebrant invites the first family to approach the font. In addition, using the name of the individual child, he asks the parents and godparents:

Is it your will, therefore, that N. should receive Baptism in the faith of the Church, which we have all professed with you?

Parents and godparents:

It is.

And immediately the celebrant baptizes the child, saying:

N., I BAPTIZE YOU IN THE NAME OF THE FATHER,

He immerses the child or pours water over him (her) a first time.

AND OF THE SON,

He immerses the child or pours water over him (her) a second time.

AND OF THE HOLY SPIRIT.

He immerses the child or pours water over him (her) a third time.

He asks the same question and does the same for each child to be baptized.

After the Baptism of each child, it is appropriate for the people to sing a short acclamation, such as:

Blessed be God, who chose you in Christ.

Other optional acclamations, nos. 225–245.

If the Baptism is celebrated by the pouring of water, it is preferable for the child to be held by the mother (or by the father); however, where it is felt that the existing custom should be retained, the child may be held by the godmother (or by the godfather). If the Baptism is by immersion, the child is lifted from the sacred font by the same person.

286. If there are many children to be baptized, and there are several Priests or Deacons present, each of them may baptize some of the children, by using the same method and formula described above.

Explanatory Rites

Anointing after Baptism

287. Then the celebrant says:

**Almighty God, the Father of our Lord Jesus Christ,
has freed you from sin,
given you new birth by water and the Holy Spirit,
and joined you to his people.
He now anoints you with the Chrism of salvation,
so that you may remain members of Christ,
      Priest, Prophet and King,
unto eternal life.**

All:

Amen.

Then, without saying anything, the celebrant anoints each baptized child with sacred Chrism on the crown of his (her) head.

If there are a large number of baptized children and there are several Priests or Deacons present, each of them may anoint some of the children with Chrism.

Clothing with a White Garment

288. The celebrant says:

**(N. and N.,) you have become a new creation
and have clothed yourselves in Christ.
May this white garment be a sign to you of your Christian dignity.
With your family and friends to help you by word and example,
bring it unstained into eternal life.**

All:

Amen.

And a white garment is placed on each child; another color is not permitted, unless it is demanded by local custom. It is desirable that the families themselves provide this garment.

Handing On of a Lighted Candle

289. The celebrant then takes the paschal candle and says:

Receive the light of Christ.

One member of each family (e.g., the father or godfather) lights a candle for each child from the paschal candle.

Then the celebrant says:

Parents and godparents,
this light is entrusted to you to be kept burning brightly,
so that your children, enlightened by Christ,
may walk always as children of the light
and, persevering in the faith,
may run to meet the Lord when he comes
with all the Saints in the heavenly court.

"Ephphatha"

290. In the United States, the "Ephphatha" Rite takes place at the discretion of the celebrant. The celebrant touches the ears and mouth of each child with his thumb, saying:

May the Lord Jesus,
who made the deaf to hear and the mute to speak,
grant that you may soon receive his word with your ears
and profess the faith with your lips,
to the glory and praise of God the Father.

All:

Amen.

291. If there are many children, the celebrant says the formula once, omitting the touching of the ears and mouth.

292. When the celebration of Baptism is concluded, the candles are set aside, all return to their places, and the Mass continues as usual with the Offertory.

In the Eucharistic Prayer, proper formulas from the Ritual Mass "For the Conferral of Baptism" are used.

The Concluding Rites

Blessing and Dismissal

293. For imparting the blessing at the end of Mass, the Priest may use one of the formulas which are given for the rite of Baptism.

The Priest, facing the people and extending his hands, says:

The Lord be with you.

The people reply:

And with your spirit.

The Deacon or, in his absence, the Priest himself, says the invitation:

Bow down for the blessing.

Then the Priest, with hands extended over the people, blesses the mothers, holding their children in their arms, the fathers, and all those present, saying:

The Lord God Almighty,
through his Son, born of the Virgin Mary,
brings joy to Christian mothers
as the hope of eternal life shines forth upon their children.
May he graciously bless the mothers of these children,
so that, as they now give thanks for the gift of their children,
they may always remain united with them in thanksgiving,
in Christ Jesus our Lord.

All:

Amen.

Celebrant:

May the Lord God Almighty,
the giver of life both in heaven and on earth,
bless the fathers of these children,
so that, together with their wives,
they may, by word and example,
prove to be the first witnesses of the faith to their children,
in Christ Jesus our Lord.

All:

Amen.

Celebrant:

**May the Lord God Almighty,
who by water and the Holy Spirit
has given us new birth into eternal life,
abundantly bless his faithful here present,
that always and everywhere they may be active members
        of his people;
and may he bestow his peace on all who are here,
in Christ Jesus our Lord.**

All:

Amen.

Celebrant:

**May almighty God bless you,
the Father, and the Son, ✝ and the Holy Spirit.**

All:

Amen.

Other optional formulas of blessing, nos. 247–249.

294. Then the Deacon, or the Priest himself, with hands joined and facing the people, says:

Go forth, the Mass is ended.

Or:

Go and announce the Gospel of the Lord.

Or:

Go in peace, glorifying the Lord by your life.

Or:

Go in peace.

The people reply:

Thanks be to God.

295. Then the Priest venerates the altar as usual with a kiss, as at the beginning. After making a profound bow with the ministers, he withdraws.

OUTLINE OF THE RITE

THE INTRODUCTORY RITES

Rite of Receiving the Child
Procession to the Altar
(Glory to God in the Highest)
Collect Prayer

THE LITURGY OF THE WORD

Biblical Readings and Homily
Universal Prayer (Prayer of the Faithful)
  and Litany
Prayer of Exorcism
  (and Anointing before Baptism)
Procession to the Place of Baptism

CELEBRATION OF BAPTISM

Blessing of Water and Invocation of God
  over the Water
Renunciation of Sin and Profession of Faith
Baptism

EXPLANATORY RITES

Anointing after Baptism
Clothing with a White Garment
Handing On of a Lighted Candle
("Ephphatha")

THE LITURGY OF THE EUCHARIST

THE CONCLUDING RITES

Blessing and Dismissal

ORDER OF BAPTISM FOR ONE CHILD WITHIN MASS

THE INTRODUCTORY RITES

RITE OF RECEIVING THE CHILD

296. When the people are gathered, they sing the Entrance Chant or a suitable Psalm or hymn, if circumstances allow. Meanwhile, the Priest celebrant, wearing vestments with the color proper to the day or the liturgical time, or with the color white or a festive color on days when Ritual Masses are permitted, goes with the ministers to the door of the church, or to that part of the church where the parents and godparents are gathered with the child.

297. When the Entrance Chant is concluded, the Priest and the faithful, standing, sign themselves with the Sign of the Cross, while the Priest says:

In the name of the Father, and of the Son, and of the Holy Spirit.

The people reply:

Amen.

298. The Greeting and Penitential Act from the *Roman Missal* are omitted. Instead, the celebrant greets those present, especially the parents and godparents, recalling in a few words the joy with which the parents received their child as a gift from God, who is the source of all life and who now wishes to bestow his own life on him (her). He may use these or similar words:

Dear parents and godparents:
Your family has experienced great joy at the birth of your child,
and the Church shares your happiness.
Today this joy has brought you to the Church
to give thanks to God for the gift of your child
and to celebrate a new birth in the waters of Baptism.

This community rejoices with you,
for today the number of those baptized in Christ will be increased,
and we offer you our support in raising your child
in the practice of the faith.
Therefore, brothers and sisters,
let us now prepare ourselves to participate in this celebration,
listening to God's Word, praying for this child and his (her) family,
and renewing our commitment to the Lord and to his people.

299. The celebrant first asks the parents of the child:

What name do you give (or: have you given) your child?

Parents:

N.

Celebrant:

What do you ask of God's Church for N.?

Parents:

Baptism.

The celebrant may use other words in this dialogue.

The first reply may be given by another person if, according to local custom, this person has the right to give the name.

In the second reply, the parents may use other words: e.g., Faith or The grace of Christ or Entry into the Church or Eternal life.

300. Then the celebrant addresses the parents in these or similar words:

In asking for Baptism for your child,
you are undertaking the responsibility
of raising him (her) in the faith,
so that, keeping God's commandments,
he (she) may love the Lord and his (her) neighbor as Christ
      has taught us.
Do you understand this responsibility?

Parents:

We do.

301. Then turning to the godparents, the celebrant asks in these or similar words:

Are you ready to help the parents of this child in their duty?

Godparents:

We are (I am).

302. Then the celebrant continues, saying:

N., the Church of God receives you with great joy.
In her name I sign you with the Sign of the Cross
of Christ our Savior;
then, after me, your parents (and godparents) will do the same.

And, without saying anything, he signs the child on the forehead. Afterwards he invites the parents, and if it seems appropriate, the godparents, to do the same.

303. The procession to the altar then takes place in the customary manner. If circumstances permit, the procession takes place with singing (e.g., Psalm 85 [84]:7–9ab).

Psalm 85 (84):7–9ab

Will you not restore again our life,
    that your people may rejoice in you?
Show us, O LORD, your mercy,
    and grant us your salvation.
I will hear what the LORD God speaks;
    he speaks of peace for his people and his faithful.

304. The Priest approaches the altar with the ministers. When he has arrived at the altar, after making a profound bow with the ministers, the Priest venerates the altar with a kiss and, if appropriate, incenses the cross and the altar. Then, with the ministers, he goes to the chair.

305. Then, when it is prescribed, this hymn is either sung or said:

Glory to God in the highest,
and on earth peace to people of good will.
We praise you,
we bless you,
we adore you,
we glorify you,
we give you thanks for your great glory,
Lord God, heavenly King,
O God, almighty Father.

Lord Jesus Christ, Only Begotten Son,
Lord God, Lamb of God, Son of the Father,
you take away the sins of the world,
    have mercy on us;
you take away the sins of the world,
receive our prayer;
you are seated at the right hand of the Father,
    have mercy on us.

For you alone are the Holy One,
you alone are the Lord,
you alone are the Most High,
Jesus Christ,
with the Holy Spirit,
in the glory of God the Father.
Amen.

306. When this hymn is concluded, the Priest, with hands joined, says:

Let us pray.

And all pray in silence with the Priest for a while. Then the Priest, with hands extended, says the Collect prayer. The Collect of the day is used, but on days when Ritual Masses are permitted, one of the following prayers is said:

O God, who bring us to participate in the mystery
of the Passion and Resurrection of your Son,
grant, we pray,
that, strengthened by the spirit of adoption as your children,
we may always walk in newness of life.
Through our Lord Jesus Christ, your Son,
who lives and reigns with you in the unity of the Holy Spirit,
one God, for ever and ever.

All:

Amen.

Or:

O God, who bring us to rebirth by the word of life,
grant that, accepting it with a sincere heart,
we may be eager to live by the truth
and may bear abundant fruits of fraternal charity.
Through our Lord Jesus Christ, your Son,
who lives and reigns with you in the unity of the Holy Spirit,
one God, for ever and ever.

All:

Amen.

The Liturgy of the Word

Biblical Readings and Homily

307. The celebrant invites the parents, godparents, and others present to take part in the Liturgy of the Word.

The Liturgy of the Word is celebrated in the usual manner. At Sunday Masses, the readings are taken from the Mass of the day. During Christmas Time and Ordinary Time, and at weekday Masses, they may also be taken from those which are given in the *Lectionary for Mass* (nos. 756–760) or in this Order (nos. **44**, **186–215**).

When a Ritual Mass is not permitted, one of the readings may be taken from the texts provided for the Baptism of children, having due regard for the pastoral needs of the faithful and the character of the liturgical day.

308. After the Readings, the celebrant preaches the Homily, which is based on the sacred text, but should take into consideration the Baptism being celebrated.

309. After the Homily, it is recommended that there be a period of silence in which all, invited by the celebrant, pray in their hearts.

The Creed is not said, because its place is taken by the profession of faith, which is made by the entire community before the Baptism.

Universal Prayer (Prayer of the Faithful)

310. The Universal Prayer (Prayer of the Faithful) is taken from those in the *Order of Baptism*. At the end, however, before the invocation of the Saints, petitions are added for the universal Church and for the needs of the world.

Celebrant:

Dear brothers and sisters,
let us invoke the mercy of our Lord Jesus Christ
for this child about to receive the grace of Baptism,
and for his (her) parents, godparents, and all the baptized.

**Give this child new birth in Baptism
through the radiant divine mystery of your Death and Resurrection,
and join him (her) to your holy Church:**

All:

Lord, we ask you, hear our prayer.

Lector:

**Make him (her) a faithful disciple and witness to your Gospel
through Baptism and Confirmation:**

All:

Lord, we ask you, hear our prayer.

Lector:

**Lead him (her) through holiness of life
to the joys of the heavenly Kingdom:**

All:

Lord, we ask you, hear our prayer.

Lector:

**Make his (her) parents and godparents
a shining example of the faith to this child:**

All:

Lord, we ask you, hear our prayer.

Lector:

Keep his (her) family always in your love:

All:

Lord, we ask you, hear our prayer.

Renew the grace of Baptism in each of us:

Lord, we ask you, hear our prayer.

Other optional formulas, nos. 217–220.

311. Afterwards, the celebrant invites those present to invoke the aid of the Saints:

Holy Mary, Mother of God,	pray for us.
Saint John the Baptist,	pray for us.
Saint Joseph,	pray for us.
Saint Peter and Saint Paul,	pray for us.

It is good to add the names of other Saints, especially the Patron Saint of the child or of the church or of the place. Then the Litany concludes:

All holy men and women, Saints of God,	pray for us.

Optional extended form of the Litany, no. 220A.

Prayer of Exorcism and Anointing before Baptism

312. After the invocations, the celebrant says:

Almighty ever-living God,
who sent your Son into the world
to drive out from us the power of Satan, the spirit of evil,
and bring the human race, rescued from darkness,
into the marvelous Kingdom of your light:
we humbly beseech you
to free this child from Original Sin,
to make him (her) the temple of your glory,
and to grant that your Holy Spirit may dwell in him (her).
Through Christ our Lord.

All:

Amen.

Another formula for the Prayer of Exorcism, no. 221.

313. The celebrant continues:

May the strength of Christ the Savior protect you.
As a sign of this we anoint you with the oil of salvation
in the same Christ our Lord,
who lives and reigns for ever and ever.

> All:

Amen.

> The celebrant anoints the child on the breast with the Oil of Catechumens.

> 314. In the United States, if, for serious reasons, the celebrant judges it pastorally necessary or desirable, the Anointing before Baptism may be omitted. In that case, the celebrant says:

May the strength of Christ the Savior protect you;
who lives and reigns for ever and ever.

> All:

Amen.

> And immediately, without saying anything, he lays his hand on the child.

> 315. Then they proceed to the baptistery, or, if circumstances suggest, to the sanctuary, if the Baptism is celebrated there.

> Meanwhile, if it can be done with dignity, a suitable liturgical song is sung, e.g., Psalm 23 (22).

> Psalm 23 (22)

The LORD is my shepherd;
> there is nothing I shall want.
Fresh and green are the pastures
> where he gives me repose.
Near restful waters he leads me;
> he revives my soul.

He guides me along the right path,
    for the sake of his name.
Though I should walk in the valley of the shadow of death,
    no evil would I fear, for you are with me.
Your crook and your staff will give me comfort.

You have prepared a table before me
    in the sight of my foes.
My head you have anointed with oil;
    my cup is overflowing.

Surely goodness and mercy shall follow me
    all the days of my life.
In the LORD's own house shall I dwell
    for length of days unending.

CELEBRATION OF BAPTISM

316. When they have come to the font, the celebrant briefly reminds those present of the wonderful plan of God, who willed to sanctify the human soul and body through water. He may do this in these or similar words:

Let us pray, dear brothers and sisters,
that the Lord God Almighty may bestow new life on this child
by water and the Holy Spirit.

Or:

Dear brothers and sisters,
you know that God graciously bestows
his abundant life through the sacrament of water
on those who believe.
Let us then raise our minds to him,
and with one heart pray
that he may be pleased to pour out his grace from this font
upon this chosen one.

317.   Then, turning to the font, the celebrant says the following Blessing (outside Easter Time):

O God, who by invisible power
accomplish a wondrous effect
through sacramental signs
and who in many ways have prepared water, your creation,
to show forth the grace of Baptism;

O God, whose Spirit
in the first moments of the world's creation
hovered over the waters,
so that the very substance of water
would even then take to itself the power to sanctify;

O God, who by the outpouring of the flood
foreshadowed regeneration,
so that from the mystery of one and the same element of water
would come an end to vice and a beginning of virtue;

O God, who caused the children of Abraham
to pass dry-shod through the Red Sea,
so that the chosen people,
set free from slavery to Pharaoh,
would prefigure the people of the baptized;

O God, whose Son,
baptized by John in the waters of the Jordan,
was anointed with the Holy Spirit,
and, as he hung upon the Cross,
gave forth water from his side along with blood,
and after his Resurrection, commanded his disciples:
"Go forth, teach all nations, baptizing them
in the name of the Father and of the Son and of the Holy Spirit,"
look now, we pray, upon the face of your Church
and graciously unseal for her the fountain of Baptism.

May this water receive by the Holy Spirit
the grace of your Only Begotten Son,
so that human nature, created in your image
and washed clean through the Sacrament of Baptism
from all the squalor of the life of old,
may be found worthy to rise to the life of newborn children
through water and the Holy Spirit.

The celebrant touches the water with his right hand and continues:

May the power of the Holy Spirit,
O Lord, we pray,
come down through your Son
into the fullness of this font,
so that all who have been buried with Christ
by Baptism into death
may rise again to life with him.
Who lives and reigns for ever and ever.

All:

Amen.

Other optional formulas, nos. 223–224.

318. During Easter Time, however, if the baptismal water has been consecrated at the Easter Vigil, so that the Baptism may not lack the element of thanksgiving and petition, the blessing and invocation of God over the water takes place in accordance with the formulas found in nos. 223–224, using the textual variation given at the end of these same formulas.

319. The celebrant instructs the parents and godparents in these words:

Dear parents and godparents:
through the Sacrament of Baptism
the child you have presented
is about to receive from the love of God
new life by water and the Holy Spirit.

For your part, you must strive to bring him (her) up in the faith,
so that this divine life may be preserved from the contagion of sin,
and may grow in him (her) day by day.

If your faith makes you ready to accept this responsibility,
then, mindful of your own Baptism,
renounce sin and profess faith in Christ Jesus,
the faith of the Church,
in which children are baptized.

The celebrant also invites the entire community to join in the renunciation of sin and profession of faith.

320. Then the celebrant questions them:

Do you renounce Satan?

Parents, godparents, and all present:

I do.

Celebrant:

And all his works?

Parents, godparents, and all present:

I do.

Celebrant:

And all his empty show?

Parents, godparents, and all present:

I do.

Or:

Celebrant:

Do you renounce sin,
so as to live in the freedom of the children of God?

Parents, godparents, and all present:

I do.

Celebrant:

Do you renounce the lure of evil,
so that sin may have no mastery over you?

Parents, godparents, and all present:

I do.

Celebrant:

Do you renounce Satan,
the author and prince of sin?

Parents, godparents, and all present:

I do.

In the United States, if the occasion requires, this second formula may be adapted with more precision by the Diocesan Bishop, especially when it is necessary that the parents and godparents should renounce superstitions, divinations, and magical arts practiced with reference to the child.

321. Next, the celebrant elicits the threefold profession of faith by the parents and godparents, and by the entire community, saying:

Do you believe in God,
the Father almighty,
Creator of heaven and earth?

Parents, godparents, and all present:

I do.

**Do you believe in Jesus Christ, his only Son, our Lord,
who was born of the Virgin Mary,
suffered death and was buried,
rose again from the dead
and is seated at the right hand of the Father?**

Parents, godparents, and all present:

I do.

Celebrant:

**Do you believe in the Holy Spirit,
the holy catholic Church,
the communion of saints,
the forgiveness of sins,
the resurrection of the body,
and life everlasting?**

Parents, godparents, and all present:

I do.

322. The celebrant, together with the community, gives assent to this profession of faith, saying:

**This is our faith. This is the faith of the Church.
We are proud to profess it in Christ Jesus our Lord.**

All:

Amen.

Another formula may be substituted, if circumstances suggest. Or a suitable liturgical song, by which the community expresses its faith with one voice, may be sung.

323. The celebrant invites the family to approach the font. In addition, using the name of the child, he asks the parents and godparents:

Is it your will, therefore, that N. should receive Baptism in the faith of the Church, which we have all professed with you?

Parents and godparents:

It is.

And immediately the celebrant baptizes the child, saying:

N., I BAPTIZE YOU IN THE NAME OF THE FATHER,

He immerses the child or pours water over him (her) a first time.

AND OF THE SON,

He immerses the child or pours water over him (her) a second time.

AND OF THE HOLY SPIRIT.

He immerses the child or pours water over him (her) a third time.

After the Baptism of the child, it is appropriate for the people to sing a short acclamation, such as:

Blessed be God, who chose you in Christ.

Other optional acclamations, nos. 225–245.

If the Baptism is celebrated by the pouring of water, it is preferable for the child to be held by the mother (or by the father); however, where it is felt that the existing custom should be retained, the child may be held by the godmother (or by the godfather). If the Baptism is by immersion, the child is lifted from the sacred font by the same person.

Explanatory Rites

Anointing after Baptism

324. Then the celebrant says:

Almighty God, the Father of our Lord Jesus Christ,
has freed you from sin,
given you new birth by water and the Holy Spirit,
and joined you to his people.
He now anoints you with the Chrism of salvation,
so that you may remain as a member of Christ,
  Priest, Prophet and King,
unto eternal life.

  All:

Amen.

  Then, without saying anything, the celebrant anoints the child with
  sacred Chrism on the crown of his (her) head.

Clothing with a White Garment

325. The celebrant says:

N., you have become a new creation
and have clothed yourself in Christ.
May this white garment be a sign to you of your Christian dignity.
With your family and friends to help you by word and example,
bring it unstained into eternal life.

  All:

Amen.

  And a white garment is placed on the child; another color is not permitted, unless it is demanded by local custom. It is desirable that the
  family itself provide this garment.

Handing On of a Lighted Candle

326. The celebrant then takes the paschal candle and says:

Receive the light of Christ.

One member of the family (e.g., the father or godfather) lights a candle for the child from the paschal candle.

Then the celebrant says:

Parents and godparents,
this light is entrusted to you to be kept burning brightly,
so that your child, enlightened by Christ,
may walk always as a child of the light
and, persevering in the faith,
may run to meet the Lord when he comes
with all the Saints in the heavenly court.

"Ephphatha"

327. In the United States, the "Ephphatha" Rite takes place at the discretion of the celebrant. The celebrant touches the ears and mouth of the child with his thumb, saying:

May the Lord Jesus,
who made the deaf to hear and the mute to speak,
grant that you may soon receive his word with your ears
and profess the faith with your lips,
to the glory and praise of God the Father.

All:

Amen.

328. When the celebration of Baptism is concluded, the candle is set aside, all return to their places, and the Mass continues as usual with the Offertory.

In the Eucharistic Prayer, proper formulas from the Ritual Mass "For the Conferral of Baptism" are used.

The Concluding Rites

Blessing and Dismissal

329. For imparting the blessing at the end of Mass, the Priest may use one of the formulas which are given for the rite of Baptism.

The Priest, facing the people and extending his hands, says:

The Lord be with you.

The people reply:

And with your spirit.

The Deacon or, in his absence, the Priest himself, says the invitation:

Bow down for the blessing.

Then the Priest, with hands extended over the people, blesses the mother, holding her child in her arms, the father, and all those present, saying:

The Lord God Almighty,
through his Son, born of the Virgin Mary,
brings joy to Christian mothers
as the hope of eternal life shines forth upon their children.
May he graciously bless the mother of this child,
so that, as she now gives thanks for the gift of her child,
she may always remain united with him (her) in thanksgiving,
in Christ Jesus our Lord.

All:

Amen.

Celebrant:

May the Lord God Almighty,
the giver of life both in heaven and on earth,
bless the father of this child,
so that, together with his wife,
they may, by word and example,
prove to be the first witnesses of the faith to their child,
in Christ Jesus our Lord.

All:

Amen.

Celebrant:

May the Lord God Almighty,
who by water and the Holy Spirit
has given us new birth into eternal life,
abundantly bless his faithful here present,
that always and everywhere they may be active members
**   of his people;**
and may he bestow his peace on all who are here,
in Christ Jesus our Lord.

All:

Amen.

Celebrant:

May almighty God bless you,
the Father, and the Son, ✝ and the Holy Spirit.

All:

Amen.

Other optional formulas of blessing, nos. 247–249.

330. Then the Deacon, or the Priest himself, with hands joined and facing the people, says:

Go forth, the Mass is ended.

Or:

Go and announce the Gospel of the Lord.

Or:

Go in peace, glorifying the Lord by your life.

Or:

Go in peace.

The people reply:

Thanks be to God.

331. Then the Priest venerates the altar as usual with a kiss, as at the beginning. After making a profound bow with the ministers, he withdraws.

COLOPHON

For Baptism, as is proclaimed in the prayers for the blessing of water, is the washing of regeneration of the children of God and of birth from on high. The invocation of the Most Holy Trinity over those who are to be baptized has the effect that, signed with this name, they are consecrated to the Trinity and enter into fellowship with the Father, and the Son, and the Holy Spirit.

—*Christian Initiation*: General Introduction, 5

Through the waters of Baptism, a new Christian enters into relationship with God—Father, Son, and Holy Spirit. This relationship, or divine dance, extends to all the Christian encounters, for by this sacramental initiation, the newly baptized has committed to being like Christ in the world. The beautiful cover design of this ritual book reflects the diversity of the Church and evokes influences from Hispanic, Greek, and Celtic art. It symbolically depicts the many theological meanings of Baptism. Representing the waters of the font are spiral waves surrounding concentric rows of triangular tile. The three rows correspond to the Triune God as well as to the number of times the person is immersed in the reconciling waters. The tiles provide a visual effect that calls to mind descending and ascending steps within many immersion fonts, thus symbolizing that through Baptism, a person dies and rises with Christ Jesus. The circular nature of the font represents both an immersion font and the unity that Baptism forms with God and other baptized Christians. The center of the font is a triple spiral. It reminds us that Baptism is an encounter with the Triune God, and the spirals point to the waters of the font. The concentric inner bands were inspired by an eighteenth-century Ethiopian brass cross. The wave pattern was inspired by the immersion font in St. Paul the Apostle Catholic Church in Westerville, Ohio.

This edition of the *Order of Baptism of Children* displays the ritual and Scripture texts with dignity and clarity for those who proclaim them and those who listen to them. The design eliminates page-turns wherever possible, and the use of two colors differentiates rubrics from what is to be proclaimed. The line length for the prayer texts and Scripture readings gives a pleasing proportion to the page as a whole and assists the reader in public proclamation of the text. Its design and layout represents an effort by Liturgy Training Publications to provide parish ministers with a dignified ritual book that helps to incorporate new Christians into the life of the Church. The cover was designed by Anna Manhart. The interior was designed by Mark Hollopeter.

The type is set in Goudy Old Style created in 1915 by Frederic W. Goudy for American Type Founders.

The text is printed in black and PMS red 200U inks on acid-free 60#
Domtar Lynx Opaque White paper to prevent discoloration over time.

The front cover and spine are stamped in silver foil. The cover material,
Rainbow LX with Vicuna embossing, was made by Ecological Fibers with
environmentally-sound manufacturing processes. The endsheet material is 80#
Navy Rainbow with Felt embossing, a durable paper that also was made by
Ecological Fibers.

The two ribbon markers are ⅜" wide grosgrain in Century Blue and Antique
White.

The book block is Smyth sewn, and the spine is round-backed, providing
a durable ritual book that can be used daily for multiple celebrations of the baptismal rites.

This book was printed and bound in the United States of America.